D0301528

Making Public Private Partnerships Work

Building Relationships and Understanding Cultures

MICHAEL GEDDES

GOWER

Published by
Gower Publishing Limited
Gower House
Croft Road
Aldershot
Hants GU11 3HR
England

Gower Publishing Company
Suite 420
101 Cherry Street
Burlington,
VT 05401-4405
USA

Michael Geddes has asserted his right under the Copyright, Designs and Patents Act 1988 to be identified as the author of this work.

British Library Cataloguing in Publication Data
Geddes, Michael
   Making public private partnerships work: building
   relationships and understanding cultures
   1. Public-private sector cooperation – Great Britain
   2. Partnership - Great Brritain
   I. Title
   338.7'3'0941

   ISBN 0 566 08645 X

Library of Congress Cataloging-in-Publication Data
Geddes, Michael.
   Making public private partnerships work: building relationships
and understanding cultures / Michael Geddes.
        p. cm.
   Includes bibliographical references.
   ISBN 0-566-08645-X
   1. Public-private sector cooperation -- Great Britain. 2. Industrial
   policy -- Great Britain.
I. Title.

   HD3616. G7G43 2005
   361.2'5'0941 -- dc 22

                                                                2005046000

Typeset by IML Typographers, Birkenhead, Merseyside.
Printed and bound in Great Britain by TJ International Ltd, Padstow, Cornwall.

Contents

List of Figures   *vii*

List of Case Studies   *viii*

Acknowledgements   *ix*

1 Context and the Nature of Public Private Partnerships   **1**

Historical background   2

Sectoral cultural differences   6

Categories of public private partnerships   8

Summary   15

2 Partnership Development Process and Identification of a Champion   **17**

Partnership lifecycle   17

Partnership establishment process   20

Partnership drivers   24

Identification of a partnership champion   27

Interim organizational structure   31

Summary   34

3 Partnership Development Strategy: Characteristics of Possible Partners   **35**

Key sectors – appropriate approaches   36

Developing a stakeholder map   44

Negotiation process   46

Summary   48

4 Partnership Development Strategy: Organizational Structure   **49**

An informal partnership   50

A formal partnership   51

Company structure   52

Making the choice   54

Summary   59

5 Partnership Development Strategy: Governance, Resources and Staffing   **61**

Membership   61

Role and appointment of the chair   66
The powers and functions of the board   69
Infrastructure to support the PPP   73
Resourcing a partnership   76
Summary   77

6 Managing a Partnership's Business   79
Underlying principles   80
Business management process   81
A PPP's strategic plan   84
A PPP's annual business plan   86
Operational management   88
Summary   93

7 Accountability and Keeping in Touch   95
Types of accountability   96
Keeping in touch   103
Summary   109

8 Setting Targets and Measuring Success   111
Aim of target-setting process   112
Target setting applied to PPPs   113
Characteristics of targets   116
Target reporting system   119
Summary   121

9 Characteristics of Successful Partnerships   123
Purpose and objectives   124
Leadership quality   125
Partnership values   126
Operational and management structures   128

References   *133*
Index   *135*

List of Figures

1.1	The development of Public Private Partnerships	7
1.2	PPP categories	14
2.1	Partnership lifecycle	19
2.2	Potential partners power/energy matrix	25
2.3	Identifying a partnership champion	28
2.4	Role of partnership champion	28
3.1	A possible stakeholder map for developing a PPP on economic development	45
4.1	Organizational options for a PPP	56
5.1	Membership of a PPP	63
5.2	Options for a PPP board	71
6.1	Confidence level in a PPP	79
6.2	Components of a PPP's business plan	89
7.1	PPP accountability	97
7.2	Elements of a communication strategy	104
8.1	PPP value for money	115
8.2	Characteristics of targets	117
9.1	Characteristics of successful partnerships	131

List of Case Studies

Partnerships as a way of thinking 4
Developing a partnership takes time 19
Rationale for a PPP 22
The partnership development process – steering groups and champions 32
Developing an appropriate organizational structure 57
Classification of stakeholders 65
The role and appointment of a PPP's chair 68
The nature and powers of a partnership board 70
The executive leadership and staffing of partnerships 75
Developing strategic and annual business plans 89
Structures to support a partnership board 91
Maintaining acccounability and keeping in touch 107
Establishing targets and measuring success 116

Acknowledgements

I became involved in the world of public private partnerships in the mid-1990s when I was appointed the part-time Executive Director of the Milton Keynes Economic Partnership with a brief to convert the initial ideas into a realistic concept. The partnership became one of the first economic partnerships in the UK and I am very grateful to all those who helped in that process. I would particularly like to thank the first chairman David Winks and Vanessa Gwynn from Milton Keynes Council but all of those involved deserve credit and my gratitude. I would also like to thank my colleagues in the wider South East family of partnerships which has grown up over the last ten years or so and to record my appreciation of the open way in which they have shared experiences and information. The book itself would not have been possible without the active help of Lorraine Oliver and her colleagues in the Learning Resource Centre at Ashridge Management College. My limited mastery of the keyboard is a tribute to the patience and technical knowledge of Arthur Christian who has been invaluable. Finally I would like to acknowledge with thanks the support and encouragement of my wife Leslie who has had to suffer the inevitable tantrums of an author!

CHAPTER 1

Context and the Nature of Public Private Partnerships

The Oxford Dictionary defines a 'partnership' as a 'joint business with shared risks and profits'; this somewhat narrow definition is expanded in Roget's Thesaurus which includes as related nouns the words 'cooperation', 'inclusion' and 'association'. While today's public private partnerships (PPPs) are often formed to carry out a specific business task, as envisaged by the dictionary definition, they are just as frequently formed to meet the wider tasks lying behind the thesaurus suggestions. Furthermore membership of today's PPPs is no longer restricted to the traditional central government, local government and private sectors; the boundaries between the public and private sectors are now very blurred and today's partnerships involve community, educational and health groups, many of whom receive funding from both public and private sources.

The formal term 'public private partnership' only really came into common usage in the UK in the late 1990s. Prior to then, as part of the national agenda to improve the delivery of public services, there had been a great deal of discussion centring around the need for public bodies to involve other organizations in the delivery of public services; this concept of 'partnering' was encapsulated in the following definition published by the Department for the Environment, Transport and the Regions (DETR) in 1998 (Section 2: Executive Summary):

> *Partnering involves two or more organizations working together to improve performance through mutual objectives, devising a way of resolving disputes and committing to continuous improvement, measuring progress and sharing gains.*

The partnering process thus encouraged by central government led to the creation of formal public private partnerships, the first major study of which was undertaken by the Institute of Public Policy Research (IPPR); they established a Commission on Public Private Partnerships which put forward the following working definition of a PPP in their Report *Building Better Partnerships* published in June 2001:

> *A risk sharing relationship based upon a shared aspiration between the public sector and one or more partners from the private and/or voluntary sectors to deliver a publicly agreed outcome and/or public service* (Page 40).

A similar definition was put forward by a Working Group set up by the Northern Ireland Executive to review Public Private Partnerships in 2003:

> *A Public Private Partnership is generally a medium to long term relationship between the public and private sectors (including the voluntary and community sector), involving the sharing of risks and rewards and the utilisation of multi-sectoral skills, expertise and finance to deliver desired policy outcomes that are in the public interest* (Para 1.8).

These definitions highlight a number of characteristics of a PPP:

- It is a medium- to long-term relationship; it is not a 'quick fix'.
- It is a relationship based on shared aspirations.
- It can involve a range of partners.
- It involves the sharing of risks, rewards and resources on the part of all the partners.
- The aim is to deliver outcomes and services in the public interest on a continuously improving basis.

In the last few years a considerable amount has been written about the policy framework behind the creation of PPPs (the reference section at the end of this book gives details of where further information about PPPs can be found) but much of this material concentrates on partnership issues stemming from the government's efforts to improve best value in service delivery. This book builds on that work, but covers the much broader range of PPP activity that has grown up in the last few years – PPPs are now much more than just an extension of a contractual relationship. The book is about how to make multi-sector partnership working, across the whole range of PPPs, more effective in the increasingly complex world in which we now find ourselves. Because of this complexity the book cannot hope to answer all the challenges facing those now working in the PPP field; however many of the ideas and solutions which have been developed in one type of partnership can be applied to others.

HISTORICAL BACKGROUND

For many years partnership working has been espoused by government at all levels and of whatever hue. Politicians have always been happy to associate themselves with the concept of working with others but the reality, of course, is that they are very reluctant to share power with anyone else; for their part, bureaucrats, at any level, prefer obfuscation to the clarity which true partnership working requires. Thus, while partnership working has been endorsed as a 'good idea' for many years, it didn't really start to gather momentum in the UK until the 1980s; while continental Europe has moved at broadly the same pace as the UK, North America was, perhaps, slightly ahead.

In what might be called the immediate 'pre-partnership' world, government at central or local level determined policy, decided whether or not to consult others, allocated resources, and then announced the procurement process. While occasionally this process would involve different sources of finance (including private sources) in areas such as housing or regeneration, the ultimate responsibility or control was left with the relevant central or local government body. However the original command and control approach under which all public services were funded and delivered by government had been gradually modified during the 1970s and 1980s by the introduction of such concepts as 'best value' and the use of the private sector to deliver some public services under contract. Advisory or monitoring partnerships were sometimes created but there was a fairly limited amount of true partnership working; in particular, government permitted little interference in policy development. It was a fairly straightforward world (if frustrating for those invited on to 'advisory partnerships'), but it did result in a system with certain characteristics:

- It was essentially a 'big brother' approach, which assumed that government knew best; the consumers of services (or policies) – customers – had very little say or influence.

- It resulted in a fairly confrontational process between government and both the consumers and providers of services. The general public are not particularly interested in how services are delivered but are concerned to receive a good service. For their part the contractors' priority was to ensure that they covered their costs.

- As a result of the built-in confrontational characteristics of the system, costs increased because government had to spend time and money justifying itself.

- It was a fairly slow process because it generated a complex system of appeals and reviews to overcome stakeholder suspicion or opposition.

By the mid-1980s the context had changed significantly. In general terms the public sector was faced with eroding confidence in its ability to deliver services and was coming under increasing pressure to perform public services more effectively, efficiently and transparently. On the other side of the fence business leaders were coming to see the community as primary stakeholders and community building as being in the interests of their shareholders; 'corporate social responsibility' became a term which appeared more frequently in companies' annual reports. Against this general climate a number of more specific factors had increasingly come into play:

CASE STUDIES: Partnerships as a way of thinking

Long gone are the days (if they ever truly existed) when a complex public body such as a council could meet all the needs of its citizens directly. This is not so much a comment about the speed of the decision-making processes (which are, in any case, much improved as a result of the recent modernization initiatives) but a reflection on the sheer scale of the inter-dependencies now required to give effect to community leadership in any locality. Quite simply the number of players to be involved in borough-wide policy development is significant and expanding. In *Milton Keynes* for example, a unitary authority since the mid-1990s with a population of 210 000, their two-year-old Local Strategic Partnership (LSP) already has a membership of thirty-five organizations with outstanding applications to join.

So how does this all help? Milton Keynes is a very dynamic place. One of the fastest growing areas of the UK over the last thirty years, the Government has recently decided that it will double in size again over the next thirty years, approaching a population of 400 000 by 2030. There is not a body in the land which could deliver a well-rounded community of this scale working in isolation, and certainly not a democratic one. The Council has therefore wholeheartedly embraced the concept of partnership working and its commitment is reflected in the fact that it is an identified strand of its comprehensive performance assessment (CPA) programme.

Already there have been a range of successes. There are now ten strategic partnerships (in addition to the LSP and Community Safety Partnership, there are partnerships covering the areas of childcare, young people, learning, the economy, transport, health, the environment and housing) and the Council has in place a monthly liaison meeting whereby the lead officers of each of the partnerships come together to report key developments and share best practice. The meeting continuously reviews the priorities of each partnership – this facilitates cross-partnership linkages and minimizes duplication. The Council has already identified significant benefits: a more sophisticated understanding of the local operating environment, increased skill levels for the officers working across the different sectors, the opportunity to develop a more consistent set of relationships with its partner bodies, and a platform on which to showcase its credentials in open and transparent decision making. The Audit Commission will pass judgement on the efficacy of these arrangements during 2005.

In addition to committing itself to working in partnership at the strategic level, the Council has recognized that it cannot build its own supporting infrastructure services (such as IT, finance, HR and so on) at the speed and scale to meet the demands of the rapidly growing community. Accordingly the

Council decided to outsource these services by developing a service delivery partnership with a private provider. This partnership is contractually based and supported by a number of service level agreements; the private sector partner shares the Council's sites and letterheading and the two organizations have developed performance targets which meet the objectives of both partners and reflect their shared vision of how the services can be improved. The partnership celebrated its first anniversary in January 2005 and, although there have been the usual teething problems associated with the transfer of large numbers of staff, it is already clear that the level of service provided to the community has improved significantly and that, after all, is what defines effective partnership working.

- The development of policy, and subsequent projects to implement policies, was becoming a much more complicated process. It could no longer be presumed that government had the monopoly of wisdom.

- The development of sophisticated communication systems had facilitated an explosion of information. The arrival of the Internet and electronic mail revolutionized policy making.

- These two factors, in turn, fed the growth of pressure groups in the community who wanted to participate more fully in the policy making and implementation process.

- There was a genuine desire amongst politicians to decentralize the political process. At the macro level this can be seen in the debate which ultimately led to devolution and the creation of English regions. It is interesting to note that the White Paper putting forward the regional structure in 1997 was entitled *Building Partnerships for Prosperity*; furthermore the regional assemblies created as a result of the White Paper made specific provision for membership from the business, education and voluntary sectors.

- At the more local level there was an increasing recognition from both central and local government that service delivery could benefit from a more radical approach than hitherto, based on partnership between different agencies; organizations at all levels and all areas of activity were increasingly encouraged to 'think outside the box'. Indeed a number of local authorities now make reference to the importance of building appropriate partnerships in their vision or mission statements. Working in partnership became recognized as providing opportunities for improvement in services rather than as a precursor to privatization.

- Complementing this trend in service delivery was an increasing realization that, at the personal level, there was a need to improve the civic governance structure with more participation from individual citizens.

- And finally, perhaps most importantly of all, there was a recognition that the public sector could not continue to finance everything up front; nor did it have a monopoly of the necessary management skills – private money and expertize had to play a full part in the process. This had been happening for many years in some areas (particularly housing, community facilities, transport, and to some extent education and health), often through planning gain agreements, but had not really been looked at from a coordinated national perspective. The introduction of the Private Finance Initiative (PFI) in the 1990s provided a key impetus towards the development of Public Private Partnerships (albeit one based on a contractual arrangement). Money talks, and the creation of the PFI process suddenly accelerated the whole concept of partnership working. The PFI process also obliged government and the contracting organizations to start to quantify the risks involved in major projects and to assess how to underwrite such risks. This approach meant that those involved (particularly government) had to accept more clarity and transparency in their dealings, which is a precondition for successful partnership working.

- Alongside this was the increasing tendency for funding agencies, particularly the European Union, to require those bidding for support to do so under a partnership umbrella, with matching funding coming from a number of sources.

Thus, by the mid-1990s, there was an increasing willingness to recognize the benefits of sharing risks, rewards and benefits between the various sectors. In effect the partnership climate had changed significantly and true public private working and partnerships started to come into being. This trend was not confined to the UK. In a joint report published by the Economist Intelligence Unit and Andersen Consulting in 1999 (*Forging tomorrow's public-private partnerships*) the authors carried out an assessment of the relative development status of PPPs in a number of countries; this is summarized in Figure 1.1 opposite.

As can be seen from this the UK was regarded as being in the vanguard at that time; while the relative positions might have changed slightly since then, the UK remains in the forefront of developing the concept. The PPP movement is still, however, in its infancy; many organizations in all sectors remain reluctant to share power and influence despite their acceptance of the added value which PPPs can bring.

SECTORAL CULTURAL DIFFERENCES

As indicated in the opening paragraphs the traditional division between the public and private sectors has become much more blurred in the last few years. Many central

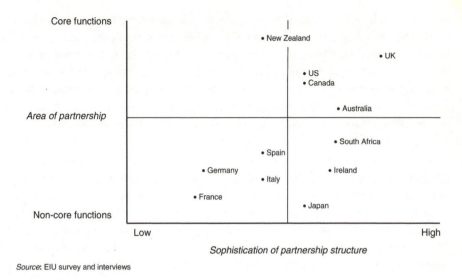

Source: EIU survey and interviews

Figure 1.1   The development of Public Private Partnerships

government agencies now 'trade' in the sense of charging for their services and have considerable financial freedom under trading fund arrangements, while many organizations in the private sector (those owned by shareholders) receive grants from government in support of their activities. Local government has become much more of a 'mixed' economy with its income made up of a mix of central grants (approx 72 per cent), a tax levied on residents (approx 20 per cent), and income from the sale of services (approx 8 per cent).

There is also a wide range of organizations which effectively sit between the public and private sectors – for example health trusts have varying degrees of freedom while still being very much in the public sector; universities are private organizations but their dependence on government funds means that their freedom of action is restricted in many ways; housing associations are in a similar position. At the same time there has been an explosion of community-based groups which receive both grant aid and charitable donations while often also running commercial sidelines. There has therefore been a considerable 'coming together' of the sectors in a financial sense. Even ownership has become more blurred with the creation of a variety of different sorts of bodies: there are commercially run organizations either owned directly or guaranteed by the government (such as the Post Office or Network Rail) or by local government (such as former direct labour organisations); there are stand-alone trusts in health and education which are theoretically independent but backed by the government.

The changing contextual and organizational landscape has had an impact on the traditional way of thinking about public services. At one end of the spectrum there

ho believed that, as a matter of principle, public services should always be
e public purse and delivered by public sector employees. This school of
eved that, by involving the private sector with its self-interested profit
tegrity of the public service would be damaged in some way; they also
believed that by having a monopoly supplier clearly accountable to a specific political
master (at either the national or local level), public services would remain
democratically driven – any watering down of this clarity would be dangerous.

At the other end of the spectrum the traditional 'privatizers' believed that, as
prosperity increased, the public would expect a much more diverse range of services
not all of which had to be provided directly by the government and for which they
would be prepared to pay extra in return for the chance to choose. They believed in
minimum government which did not need to be held to account for the full range of
services required by the public – the consumer would be an intelligent purchaser who
would drive the market operating under the normal pricing mechanism.

Neither of these two extreme viewpoints can easily accommodate the reality of a
properly functioning Public Private Partnership world. A Public Private Partnership is
a relatively new sort of animal, requiring compromises from both sets of
'traditionalists'. The PPP movement is witnessing the development of new styles of
operation and managerial control which can be uncomfortable for the individual
partners. It is not an easy exercise and it is up to the architects of the PPP process to
show that it is possible to combine the benefits of the various sectors and thus deliver a
more diverse range of services at a reasonable cost under proper accountability
arrangements. Both the organizations and (perhaps more importantly) the individuals
involved in the process have to recognize that it can only work as a mutually beneficial
exercise and have to adjust their thinking accordingly. It also has to be recognized that
the creation of a new type of organization like a PPP takes time; many years of distrust
between the sectors, with their different approaches to management and
accountability, cannot be immediately forgotten. Attitudes and philosophies take time
to change and it is likely to be some time before partnership working is accepted as the
norm.

CATEGORIES OF PUBLIC PRIVATE PARTNERSHIPS

The first wave of partnerships were mostly based on projects generated through the
PFI process where an ongoing contractual relationship was required. This was
followed by the advent of strategic service delivery partnerships at both the national
and local level, again mainly based on a contractual arrangement. The arrival of more
strategic partnerships from the end of the 1990s, which was accelerated considerably
following the election of the Labour Government in 1997, created another dimension

and it is now possible to adopt a broader and more comprehensive categorization system. A simple approach is to look at the organizational reason for the creation of a PPP. Using this approach generates three broad categories as follows:

- partnerships created as a result of legislation ('statutory based partnerships');

- partnerships created on a voluntary basis to meet a common objective ('voluntary based partnerships');

- partnerships created as a vehicle to manage the delivery of public services or projects contracted out to the private sector ('commercially or contractually based partnerships').

Adoption of this simplistic approach hides the fact that some partnerships can be defined under more than one category, but it serves as a useful tool in helping define differences in operation and style between the categories. There are however considerable commonalities amongst all those in each category, although it should be noted that the more specific nature of commercially based PPPs means that some of the features of the first two categories of partnerships (such as membership or chairmanship principles) are often not applicable to them. There are also some common principles which apply to all PPPs regardless of their categorization. In particular there is one differentiation which is common across all the categories – within each category there are two main types of PPP: those whose primary role is *strategy or policy development*, with little or no executive responsibilities; and those whose primary role is *executive action;* again, as we shall see, many partnerships combine elements of both these dimensions. This obviously affects the way a PPP is developed as will be illustrated in later chapters.

STATUTORY BASED PARTNERSHIPS

These are partnerships created as a result of a government decision or direction. Examples of these include:

Crime and Community Safety Partnerships

(Note: Some partnerships have chosen to amend this title slightly in recent years to reflect a somewhat wider role than hitherto envisaged.) The current models (of which there were 376 across England and Wales in mid-2004) have been set up under the Crime and Disorder Act 1998, and bring together the local authority and police service; most communities have added other bodies such as the fire service, the chamber of commerce, the local arm of the probation service, primary care trusts, parish council representatives and other voluntary agencies. These partnerships, and their forebears, are perhaps the first genuine statutory based PPPs and are responsible for developing strategies to address crime and disorder issues faced by the local community. The legislation provides an organizational framework and the government is allocating an increasing level of funding for specific projects which can only be spent with the approval of such partnerships. They are therefore becoming more than just a vehicle for policy development.

Local Strategic Partnerships

These were initially created to oversee the delivery of the Neighbourhood Renewal Fund (NRF); subsequently, however, the concept was extended following the enactment of the Local Government Act of 2000, Part 1 of which requires local authorities to prepare a community strategy. Subsequent government publications proposed that Local Strategic Partnerships (LSP) should oversee the preparation of that strategy. The government has not been specific on the constitution or membership of LSPs (or even the geographic coverage) leaving the details to the discretion of the local authorities. The Office of the Deputy Prime Minister (ODPM) and the Department of Transport commissioned the Universities of Warwick, West of England, and Liverpool John Moores to carry out an evaluation of LSPs in 2002, the results of which were published in 2003. They received replies from 367 local authorities which indicated that, at that time, 291 LSPs already existed (of which 87 related to areas eligible for NRF) with another 74 areas actively considering the formation of an LSP (Table 1 of the evaluation survey). The survey showed considerable variation in approach and membership across the UK but most areas appear to have adopted an inclusive approach, involving a wide range of organizations. Over 80 per cent of those who answered the question reported that the chairmanship and administrative support was provided by the local authority but this may change as LSPs mature (Tables 10 and 16 of the evaluation survey). LSPs remain primarily involved at the policy development level with very limited executive responsibilities. (Those in NRF areas are essentially supervisory in nature leaving executive action to the relevant authority.)

'Childcare' Partnerships

The title varies but the School Standards and Framework Act of 1998 requires local authorities to establish a strategic partnership to secure better services for vulnerable children. Members include the local authority and the various healthcare organizations; the voluntary sector is also represented in some areas. Partnerships of this nature have often moved from strategic coordination to the actual delivery of services.

Health/Education Action Zone Partnerships

The government, under various initiatives, has targetted specific areas for improvement in the provision of health or education services which have to be implemented jointly by the various relevant sectors including the private sector; this has led to the creation of specific PPPs with specific local objectives. Action Zone Partnerships are basically involved in policy coordination, with the actual delivery of services remaining the responsibility of the relevant authority. In mid-2004 there were 36 Health Action Zones and 47 Education Action Zones (according to the relevant websites).

Regeneration Partnerships

These are similar organizations. Again, these partnerships are a mix between policy development and service delivery.

New Deal Strategic Partnerships (and similar)

From time to time the government introduces new initiatives which the relevant government agency is required to deliver. A good example is the New Deal Programme with its various specific components; the former Employment Service and Benefits Agency (now combined) were charged with delivering the programme and were asked to set up a local partnership to help formulate a relevant local strategy. Membership usually includes the local authority, chamber of commerce and training organizations (including colleges). This type of partnership is normally chaired and administered by the delivery agency and, as the name implies, they tend to restrict themselves to policy development, leaving delivery to the relevant agency.

Transport Partnership

Some local authorities have voluntarily decided to establish partnerships to help them deliver a statutory function – for example many councils have set up a Transport Partnership which bring together the business community, the parishes, and other agencies such as the police to help the authority to develop their transport plan. It is a moot point whether such partnerships should be regarded as statutory or voluntarily based PPPs.

Local Health Forums

These are very similar bodies which have been set up in a number of areas by health authorities to help them develop statutorily required health strategies; the creation of forums enables them to involve a wide range of voluntary and community groups in their consultation process in a reasonably cost effective way without inviting them all to become members of their formal board structure. Like Transport Partnerships they are policy development vehicles with no executive function.

VOLUNTARY BASED PARTNERSHIPS

PPPs are frequently created by different organizations coming together on a voluntary basis, often in response to a government initiative. They will usually have much greater freedom in constitutional, funding and operational terms than statutory based partnerships. Examples include:

Local Economic Partnerships (or similar)

It is now recognized that it is helpful if a number of organizations (such as the local authority, the local business community, higher education, and specialist business support bodies) work together for the development of the local economy (or particular aspects thereof such as inward investment or skills development). This movement has been given considerable impetus by the government's creation of Regional Development Agencies and their requirement to produce regional economic strategies. While many economic partnerships remain primarily concerned with policy development and coordination, a number undertake executive functions (such as running an inward investment agency).

Local Learning Partnerships

These are very similar to economic partnerships although with a somewhat different membership and agenda. Again they tend to restrict their activities to policy development.

Environmentally Oriented Partnerships

A number have been established in the last few years at both regional and local levels, bringing together relevant statutory, business and voluntary organizations to produce an environmental strategy and coordinate the process of using that strategy to influence the wider economic and social agenda.

Specific service delivery coordination bodies

Local authorities, social services and health authorities are increasingly setting up multi-agency teams to coordinate the delivery of specific services; these teams often now include specialist voluntary groups and housing associations. In some areas the initial policy coordination function has been extended to include the pooling of resources and the delivery of services.

COMMERCIALLY BASED PARTNERSHIPS

A commercially based PPP is one based on a contractual relationship – a public agency, as one contracting party, contracts with one or more organizations in the private sector to deliver a particular policy, project or range of services.

Private Finance Initiative (PFI) Partnerships

Contrary to some public perception the PFI programme does not always lead to a partnership. There are two types of PFI project – firstly, those providing a capital facility only under which the private sector is invited to fund and deliver a capital project (for example a road), maintain that facility over a given time and receive a rent from the public purse. This arrangement is a purely contractual one and there is no ongoing partnership relationship. The second type of PFI project, under which the private sector provides both the capital and a range of services to operate the facility (for example a hospital where the contractor will maintain the building and provide the non-medical services) will lead to a partnership (in this case between the private sector and the relevant NHS authority). The capital cost will be recovered through the charges made for the agreed services. The partnership will be responsible for monitoring the services delivered and agreeing any changes required with the whole process governed by the underlying contract. While the initial stages of the process will have been conducted on an open tender basis, once the contractor has been identified the parties will develop the detailed specification collaboratively and agree how the services should be delivered and costed. The partnership will therefore be involved in both policy development and executive delivery.

Service Delivery Partnerships

These are very similar in nature to PFI-based partnerships except that they do not involve the initial provision of a capital facility (although the costings of the services to be delivered may include an allowance for the contractor to develop additional capital facilities – such as enhanced IT – during the course of the contract). The process by which these partnerships are created is the same as for PFI-based partnerships with the preferred bidder developing the specification in collaboration with the relevant public agency; the partnership is therefore involved in both policy development and executive delivery.

There are now a wide variety of the above two types of partnership across the public sector with an increasing range of capital facilities (hospitals, schools, community facilities and so on) and services (such as the processing of driving licences or delivery of various local services) being delivered in this way. The contractual arrangements underpinning these PPPs will specify the modus operandi of the partnership and each will have their own arrangements. Many partnerships incorporate sub-contractors or representatives of the relevant community group. There is an inevitable tension in these partnerships between the desire to work in partnership and the need to manage the relationship between the partners on a contractual basis.

There is a another type of commercially based partnership which is just starting to emerge. This is where one particular organization (normally a voluntary body or housing association) can see an advantage in inviting other sectors to help them deliver a particular 'public' project. For example a housing association may wish to involve the private sector, education sector, or local authority in helping them develop a particular geographic area. By doing so, and demonstrating a partnership approach, the housing association will then be able to attract additional resources. Another example would be where an educational body (such as a local college) creates a PPP in order to enable it to bid for particular funds. These latter partnerships are usually project based rather than policy oriented.

Figure 1.2 illustrates the current scenario. Although this is by no means a comprehensive picture it does demonstrate the increasing scale and complexity of the PPP landscape. Multi sector partnership working is rapidly becoming the norm rather than the exception.

	Statutory Based	*Voluntary Based*	*Commercially Based*
Policy Dev't	Local Strategic P'ships New Deal Strategic P'Ships	Environmental P'ships	
	Transport P'ships		
	Health Forums		
		Economic P'ships	
		Learning P'ships	
	Crime and Community P'ships		
	Childcare P'ships		
	Action Zone P'ships		
		Service Delivery P'ships	
			PFI P'ships
Service Delivery			Service Delivery P'ships

Figure 1.2   PPP categories

SUMMARY

- A multi sector partnership (PPP) is one where the partners share risks and rewards to optimize resources and skills in order to deliver a public policy.

- Since the mid-1980s there has been an increasing use of PPPs to develop and implement public policy.

- A useful way of categorizing PPPs is to do so by reference to the reason for their creation: some are created as a result of government legislation (statutory based partnerships); some are created by the members coming together voluntarily, often in response to a government initiative (voluntary based partnerships); while others are created for contractual purposes (commercially based partnerships).

- Within these categories are partnerships whose primary role is policy development, while others have a more executive orientation.

- The different nature of each PPP will require a different approach to its establishment and management, but common principles can be applied to all PPPs.

CHAPTER 2

Partnership Development Process and Identification of a Champion

PARTNERSHIP LIFECYCLE

All partnerships, of whatever category, have a natural lifecycle; they go through the following stages:

Initial concept

The initial concept will emerge from a number of sources; in the case of statutory based partnerships the concept will be set out in the relevant legislation or government publication. The concept to initiate a voluntary based partnership will also often be prompted by government action but is equally likely to arise from within one particular organization (or even from a single individual within that organization) reacting to particular circumstances. Commercially based partnerships will be created to meet a particular need, usually identified by a public agency but sometimes by an agency from another sector.

Initial refinement process

The initial concept may be fairly ill-defined (although this may not be the case in many statutory based or contractually based PPPs). There will need to be a process of refining the concept so that it can be articulated into a specific need or objective before it can be discussed more widely amongst possible stakeholders or partners.

Identification of partnership champion and interim structure

Once a consensus on the objective starts to emerge, a process to take the concept forward will need to be established. Usually an individual is identified to promote and lead the partnership development process – it will not just happen and is better left to an individual rather than a committee, although the 'champion' (or 'project manager') will need the support and help of some sort of steering group.

Development of a partnership strategy and formalization

The partnership champion's role is to develop a strategy in conjunction with the steering group: how is the overall objective to be converted into a set of specific tasks, how are partners to be involved, what sort of structures and resources are needed and so on. In the case of a contractually based partnership this phase goes further and will involve making decisions on the procurement process, that is, how to go to the market to identify a delivery partner.

Implementation of the partnership

Once a constitution has been agreed and a PPP established (or, in the case of a contractually based partnership, a contract signed) then the operation of the partnership will need to be managed; business plans have to be agreed, targets set and reporting systems put in place.

Delivery

The output and progress of the partnership will require monitoring in order to ensure that the original (or contractual) objectives are met; structures and systems need to be in place to enable the PPP to respond to changing circumstances and optimize its effectiveness.

Consequential action

PPPs set up to deliver a specific time-related task (whether of a policy development or action orientation such as the delivery of a service or services) will have a finite life time; others will have a more ill-defined timespan. In all cases however there will be consequences of the PPP's decisions or actions and these will need to be followed up and implemented.

Essentially the first four stages can be regarded as the preliminary work which requires considerable political and planning skills, while the next two stages are about the delivery process which require a different set of skills. The final stage may well lead partners back into a different phase of partnership working, with different objectives and alliances. In all partnerships there is a very real danger that insufficient time is devoted to the preliminary stages – every organization, once a new initiative (such as the establishment of a partnership) has been agreed in principle is tempted to press ahead without really thinking through the consequences. A partnership is a new type of organizational structure, the effective operation of which, by definition, brings together organizations with very different cultures and objectives, requires new approaches and the development of new attitudes. This cannot just be assumed and extra time spent on the preliminary stages considering these issues will be very well spent. Figure 2.1 expresses this diagrammatically.

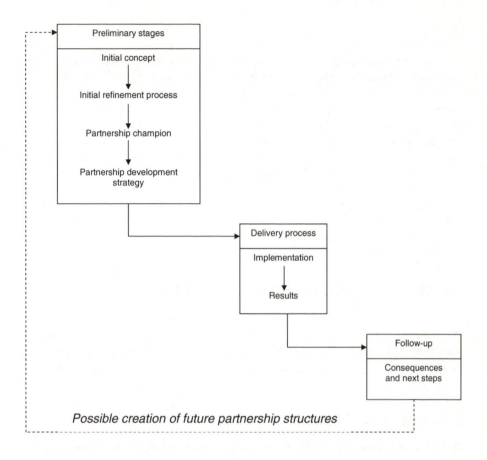

Figure 2.1 Partnership lifecycle

CASE STUDIES: Developing a partnership takes time

Because multi sector partnerships are a relatively new type of organization they take time to develop. In the case of statutory based partnerships there is often a given timescale but, as the 2002 review of Local Strategic Partnerships showed, even when there is a target date this is often not met. The review reported that 30 out of 367 local authority areas (8 per cent) had not formed a partnership after two years and some were still fairly embryonic. As far as voluntary based partnerships are concerned experience is mixed. The *Portsmouth and South East Hampshire Partnership* was formed in 1993 after a gestation period of about two years. A similar discussion period led to the establishment of the *Bedfordshire and Luton Economic Development Partnership* in 1997. It sometimes takes longer to establish a partnership – the *Kent and Medway Economic Board* grew out of an economic forum first set up in 1997; the Economic Board itself, with a wider and more comprehensive membership and remit, was established in 2001. Service delivery partnerships also take time to set up; while the principle of seeking tenders for the delivery of services can be agreed fairly quickly the practical details will determine the timescale. For example the *Milton Keynes Council* agreed to seek tenders for the delivery of its support services in early 2001; the Council then decided to invite 'open' tenders (in the sense that the tender documents set out the service areas for which tenders were sought and invited tenderers to specify which particular services they would offer and how, rather than defining the specific services in the document). As a result there was a considerable amount of subsequent negotiating time between the identification of the preferred bidder and the letting of the contract (December 2003). The Partnership came into existence in early 2004, approximately three years after the initial decision to proceed (which itself followed consideration over many months).

PARTNERSHIP ESTABLISHMENT PROCESS

Partnerships do not just happen. They are created for a purpose; furthermore all partnerships, of whatever type and for whatever purpose, undergo a similar establishment process (the first three stages of the partnership lifecycle). If a partnership is to be successful there are four factors which need to be taken into account by any organization considering participation in a partnership.

ESTABLISHMENT OF PRIMA FACIE NEED

The basic rationale for establishing a partnership will fall under five headings; generally there will be a primary reason under one of these headings, with a number of secondary reasons under other headings. It is important that those involved in establishing a PPP understand the reasons and their relative importance since this helps to inform the discussions with stakeholders and potential partners.

Public policy requirement

This is where legislation or government announcements require the creation of a PPP; it will therefore be the primary reason for the establishment of most statutory based PPPs; some voluntary based PPPs may however be created primarily for this reason (where the relevant government publication recommends the creation of a PPP but does not specify it). Public policy will also generally feature as a key secondary reason for many of the voluntary based and commercially based PPPs.

Public issues requiring a multi-agency approach

While very similar to *public policy requirement*, there are some subtle differences. The rationale for establishing a PPP may be around a specific issue which requires a multi-agency approach – for example economic development is an important broad public issue which requires the cooperation of a number of agencies; there are not, however, any statutory targets as such. While some statutory based PPPs may arise from this need, it will more often be the primary reason for the establishment of voluntary based PPPs.

Catalytic event

PPPs can be formed in response to a particular event or proposal. For example there may be a proposal to develop a community or educational facility of some sort (for example a university), and a group of organizations get together to coordinate the activity. Another example might be where a developer, in exchange for planning permission for a retail site, agrees to initiate the establishment of a PPP to coordinate the development of the relevant skills and/or related infrastructure needed for the success of the site. A number of voluntary based PPPs are formed for this purpose, and some commercially based partnerships may also be created for a specific event or opportunity.

Funding

A number of funding agencies (particularly the European Union but also some national bodies such as the Learning and Skills Council) require funding bids to come from multi sector partnerships; sometimes they specify which sectors should be involved, and occasionally the tender document also sets out the expected modus operandi of the PPP. Both voluntary based and commercially based PPPs are often formed because of funding requirements.

Synergy potential (or economic benefit)

This is usually the key reason for commercially based PPPs – the parties see considerable mutual benefits in working together. This is normally the primary reason for a council to enter into a service delivery partnership with the private sector; by utilizing the expertise and wider access to resources which a private sector contractor can offer, the council can provide a better service. The private contractor, for their part, can broaden their market and generate a better return on their assets. Essentially both partners can see significant economic benefit by working together. Partnerships set up primarily for any of the other reasons may well also see synergy potential as an important secondary benefit (via sharing of resources or expertise).

The key sponsors of a PPP need to understand both the primary and secondary reasons for establishing the partnership if they are to obtain the commitment of the potential partners. It is important that partners know, and accept, the primary

CASE STUDIES: Rationale for a PPP

The rationale for statutory based partnerships (such as LSPs or Crime and Community Safety Partnerships) is set out in the relevant legislation or government publication. Equally the rationale for commercially based partnerships is set out in the tender documents issued by the client agency – for example, when seeking to establish a partnership to take over the management of the *National Air Traffic System* (NATS) it was made clear that this was primarily for financial reasons. The government could not afford the full level of investment required but there would be opportunities for the selected partner to grow the business in the light of anticipated traffic growth and the predicted tendering of other national franchises elsewhere in Europe; however the government needed to remain the key partner with a 'golden share' for safety and security reasons. Other service delivery partnerships have similar characteristics although often there is a cost saving motivation – for example *Lincolnshire CC*, in contracting out various support services were looking for both savings and innovations in service delivery as a result of private sector management and investment. Voluntary based partnerships can be formed both for specific purposes and for more general strategic purposes. For example the *Northamptonshire Partnership* was initially formed specifically to ensure the implementation of the Regional Economic Strategy published by the East Midlands RDA; like other similar partnerships in the region it was required to seek formal accreditation from EMDA and, as a result of that accreditation, receives significant programme funds from EMDA. It does however have a wider strategic development role. On the other hand the *Buckinghamshire Economic Partnership*'s primary aim is to promote the county as a place to do business in rather than to run programmes as such. However both partnerships have adopted a very similar structure based on a company limited by guarantee with a private sector chair. *The Kent and Medway Economic Board* has amongst its objectives a specific aim 'to add value to the work of the economic development agencies'.

reason(s) for establishing a PPP; these must fit with the policy objectives of their own organization if they are to be able to secure the commitment of their colleagues; any misunderstanding can lead to subsequent difficulties. For example a partnership where the public sector involvement is primarily for public policy reasons but the private sector involvement is primarily for commercial reasons will not flourish unless the representatives of the two sectors appreciate (and respect) the other's motivation. Time spent on understanding the reasons for a PPP, and in appreciating the reasons as they apply to the potential partners, will therefore be very well worthwhile in the long run.

APPRECIATION OF WIDER CONTEXT

The prima facie need for the establishment of a PPP is generally fairly specific. Of equal concern is an understanding of the wider context within which the PPP will need to operate. PPPs, by definition, are centred around public policy issues and implementation. They are a new type of hybrid organization with very 'public' arrangements – the confidentiality which the private sector takes for granted does not feature in the PPP world (even the principal terms of a contractually based PPP will be published in the minutes of the public authority partner); the term 'open-book accounting' applies strictly speaking to financial matters but the principles behind the term apply to the full range of a partnership's work. It follows that, when developing a PPP, a number of key contextual factors need to be borne in mind:

- What will be its *symbolism* in overall political terms? How will it be seen by the wider stakeholder group (and not just those directly involved)?

- What processes and procedures need to be built in to demonstrate its *accountability* to the wider community?

- Are its expected *targets and outcomes* consistent with overall public policy in the relevant area?

- Can it be demonstrated to be a *cost effective* approach?

- Can it be seen to be adequately *inclusive* in its approach?

These are the sort of questions with which managers in the public sector are very familiar and will have to address in justifying their participation in a PPP; how to approach these issues is discussed later in this book. However they are not the sort of issue which the private sector normally has to consider and is comfortable with (apart, perhaps, from the cost effectiveness one). Private sponsors will therefore have to pay particular attention to the very public contextual nature of a PPP before they become involved.

DEVELOPMENT OF SUCCESS CRITERIA

Any enterprise needs to know where it is going and how it will measure success. This is particularly true when establishing a new enterprise such as a PPP. There has to be clarity in how success will be judged if partners from different backgrounds are to be encouraged to join. While it may be fairly easy to establish overall objectives and outcomes at the macro level, it becomes more difficult at the micro or individual partner level. A key task of the initial sponsors of a PPP is to think through an appropriate set of outcomes and success criteria which will appeal to the partners whom they hope to attract. For example local authorities will have a fairly specific agenda geared to local electoral circumstances; thus the development of an economic strategy through a voluntary based partnership will need to incorporate some specific targets (such as increasing employment amongst young people) as well as general wealth creation. Similarly, a health strategy will have a number of specific national targets but these will have to be linked to economically beneficial outcomes if the private sector is to be encouraged to join a partnership. Commercially based partnerships to deliver a PFI project or specific services will have very specific success criteria written into the contractual arrangements.

IDENTIFICATION OF INITIAL PARTNERS

The final factor influencing the partnership establishment process is the identification of potential partners. This is discussed below.

PARTNERSHIP DRIVERS

The previous section outlined key factors influencing the partnership establishment process; references in the text were made to 'the partnership sponsor'. While this term will be widely understood the unusual nature of a PPP is perhaps better served by the word 'driver'. This is because a successful PPP requires an acceptance by all partners that it is essentially independent of any single partner; it must add value to the work of all the partners and, for that reason, should not be seen as being sponsored or owned by any one partner – sponsorship implies an element of control, and control by central or local government is one of the features of the 'pre-partnership world' which partnership working seeks to change.

But a partnership cannot come into existence by itself; there has to be a driver (or drivers) of some sort who will steer the process through the initial stages of the establishment process. There are three potential categories of drivers, all of whom are likely to play a part in the initial process:

- There are likely to be one or more self evident 'founder' partners.

- There will be some fairly obvious organizations who will become involved in the partnership process early on.

- Within both of the above categories there will be a number of key individuals whose support will be essential if the PPP is to succeed.

FOUNDER PARTNERS

In many cases the identification of the founder partners will be reasonably obvious from the primary prima facie reason for a PPP. In the case of statutory based partnerships the legislation will often specify the initial partners – for example the founder partners of a

Crime and Community Safety Partnership have to be the local authority and the police service. Other statutory based partnerships will be around particular topics (such as health or housing) where the founder partners can be clearly identified. At the other end of the PPP scale the founder partners of the commercially based partnerships will also be fairly obvious – they will be the contracting parties to the initiative, for example the local authority and the private sector organization chosen to deliver the specified range of services. On the other hand, the founder partners of voluntary based PPPs can sometimes be difficult to identify although usually it will depend on the prima facie need for the PPP. The speed and robustness of the actual partner identification process will, however, be dependent on the local partnership culture.

While it is undoubtedly true that partnership working is increasingly becoming the norm, the extent to which it has been wholeheartedly adopted varies throughout the UK. In some areas the concept of partnership working is seen as crucial and is reflected in the vision statements of local organizations while in other areas there is a greater reluctance. It is noticeable that, where partnership working is a fully accepted feature, there is often cross membership of boards (between, for example, the health trusts/authorities, the voluntary sector, various educational bodies, and the chamber of commerce). The resultant individual contacts make it much easier to identify the founder partners of a potential PPP.

POTENTIAL PARTNERS

It is too simplistic to pretend that a PPP will have such clear objectives that the partners can be immediately identified without further thought. By its very nature the work of a PPP will impinge on a wide range of organizations (see comments on the contextual dimension above). Some of these affected organizations will want to play a part in the partnership establishment process; at the very minimum level they will wish to be kept informed, and they might well wish to influence the process in order to protect their interests. Figure 2.2 is a simple power/energy matrix which helps to clarify the status of potential partners.

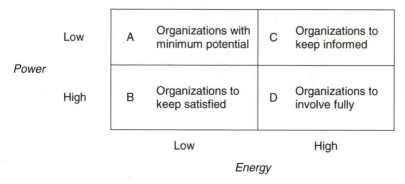

Figure 2.2 Potential partners power/energy matrix

The importance of an organization to a potential PPP is assessed in two dimensions – power and energy. The power dimension is a fairly self-evident one; it is clearly important to ensure that any powerful organization is on-side since, if they are not, they will have the ability to hinder (or possibly halt) the establishment of the PPP. The energy dimension is also important since the process of setting up a new organization such as a PPP requires effort over and above an organization's usual workload because a PPP is different (and possibly challenging). The combination of high power and energy is a potent mix.

KEY INDIVIDUALS

Organizations make decisions on the basis of the views of key individuals. The decision-making structure of every organization is specific to that organization – some are very centralized, some are very bureaucratic and so on. However, regardless of structure, there will be key individuals who initiate action, perhaps within the context of a board or committee meeting or perhaps by issuing specific instructions. The matrix in Figure 2.2 is useful in identifying potential key individuals to involve in the partnership establishment process as potential partners with, perhaps, one slight difference. While the most important category remains D as shown in the matrix, high energy is probably more important than high power at the initial stages of the establishment process. This is because the initial stages of partnership development require individual enthusiasm above all else – an enthusiast in an organization can influence others with more power, while a powerful individual will not become energized without a high level of interest.

This analysis suggests that, in order to start the partnership establishment process, there is a need to identify an appropriate individual, or group of individuals, in the relevant organizations. There are a number of different ways of doing this. Many public or statutory based organizations (such as local authorities, health authorities or chambers of commerce) employ officers specifically for the purpose of liaising with other similar bodies. Often they meet together on a regular (perhaps informal) basis – for example education or economic development officers from all the councils within a county area frequently meet together to exchange views and keep in touch. The chamber of commerce will usually have dedicated liaison officers of some sort. Some private sector companies (such as those with a large involvement in public services) may have similar individuals but most companies will not. If it is available this local network of individuals will be a very useful initial sounding board for discussion of a PPP proposal particularly of a statutory or voluntary nature. Where such networks do not exist they will have to be created by someone from one of the founder partner organizations. Local networks of this nature may not be of such importance to commercially based PPPs since companies tendering for such work will develop their own staffing structures with direct links to their opposite numbers in the relevant public bodies.

IDENTIFICATION OF A PARTNERSHIP CHAMPION

Notwithstanding the analysis set out earlier, there will inevitably be a certain lack of clarity in the initial stages of developing a PPP of whatever type. This initial stage can often take some time – for example it can take a number of years to convince local organizations that a voluntary PPP (in say the economic, transport, or learning areas) would be worthwhile exploring in principle. Statutory PPPs (which usually have an identifiable number of founder partners) will not take so long – indeed government is likely to specify a deadline – while the timescale for commercially based PPPs will usually be derived from the detailed contractual discussions.

The initial phase is often conducted on a fairly confidential basis (almost on a 'need to know' basis) for fear of antagonizing one or other potential partners or for commercial reasons. However once the initial phase is over the process has to start to become formalized and open. It would be unrealistic to hope that this next stage can be led by an informal group of officers or a committee muddling its way through. A more focused approach is necessary and experience has shown that it is more effective to identify an individual to lead the process. Indeed all the earlier studies on service delivery partnerships have emphasized the importance of this role – for example the New Local Government Network (NLGN) in their 2001 Report *Strategic Partnerships for Local Service Delivery* specifically identified the need for local authorities to appoint such an individual (Chapter 4 of the Report), while the 2004 final Report of the ODPM's Strategic Partnering Taskforce recommended that 'a dedicated full time project manager be identified at an early stage' (Section 2: Executive Summary). This individual then becomes the partnership champion and their role derives from putting together the establishment process with the partnership drivers, as shown in Figure 2.3.

As noted above in a commercially based PPP this role is usually filled by a project manager of some sort, employed initially by the relevant public authority (perhaps subsequently working in tandem with an opposite number in the private sector contractor). The need for the role may well not become immediately apparent in statutory or voluntary based PPPs – the informal discussions on the formation of a PPP may take some time. However at some stage in the development of all categories of PPPs an individual will need to take hold of the process and start to drive it forward.

The precise nature and characteristics of the role of champion will vary from partnership to partnership, but the essential core of the role will be similar in all cases

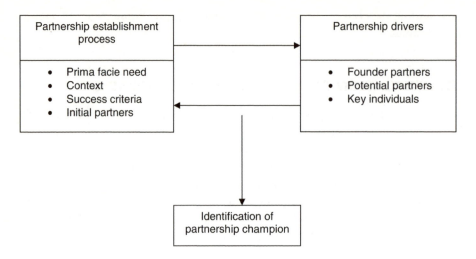

Figure 2.3   Identifying a partnership champion

and is shown diagrammatically in Figure 2.4. The champion is there to turn the partnership into reality – to produce a partnership development strategy which has the support of all the partners. This has to be done by managing three key components:

- the views of the initial drivers of the PPP;

- the views of the wider stakeholder group (all those likely to be affected by the PPP);

- the champion's own time; it is important not to forget this last element since often the champion is asked to fit this task around other commitments.

It is evident that the role of champion is crucial to the success of a PPP, yet the choice of champion is frequently rushed or just left to evolve. It is also important to remember

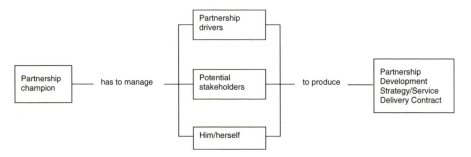

Figure 2.4   Role of partnership champion

that the champion is not necessarily the same individual who will ultimately manage or direct the partnership – the skills necessary to set up a PPP are very different from those required to run one.

The first stage in identifying a champion is to recognize the skills required. While the emphasis will clearly depend on the nature of each PPP there are certain common features:

'Local' knowledge

PPPs are 'locally' based, whether by geographic or topic coverage; the key stakeholders will be linked either by geography, by specialist knowledge or by delivery of a specific service. The champion must have a good understanding of the characteristics and strengths of the potential partners if they are to be effective from the start. Such knowledge is needed from the outset – valuable time can be lost at this stage by trying to build up local knowledge at the same time as trying to develop the PPP's strategy. Given the ever-present lack of resources in local organizations there is a tendency to appoint external consultants to develop a potential PPP's strategy but this inclination should be resisted if possible – while they may be able to offer a structured approach based on careful analysis, they may well miss crucial elements of personal expertise or influence.

Strategic vision

The champion needs to understand the broad context within which the PPP will have to operate and will be working at a fairly strategic level, certainly in the initial stages. Furthermore they will need to demonstrate an appreciation of the relationship between the strategic context and the operational functions of the potential partners in order to demonstrate the benefits of the partnership to the potential partners.

Political skills

The success of the initial stages of a PPP's strategic development will depend to a very large extent on the political skills of the champion at two levels. First of all, at the macro level, the champion will be dealing with senior individuals in the various partner organizations, many of whom may be fairly agnostic (if not hostile) to the idea of a PPP. The champion will need to demonstrate an ability to work at such a level, with good negotiating and brokering skills. There is, however, an equally important second level – the operational level. The detailed PPP development strategy (and, in the longer term, the implementation of the work of the PPP) is likely to be carried out at a more junior level in the various partners by individuals who will not necessarily have the strategic understanding of their senior colleagues; they may also be under significant day-to-day pressures. The champion has to have the skills to 'sell' the PPP concept to such staff and to persuade them to help develop the PPP strategy in ways which will benefit their own roles. The champion therefore has to have a wide range of political skills in order to operate effectively at a number of different levels within the potential partners.

Teamworking skills

No partnership can work through 'directional' leadership – the partners must feel that they are part of a team and that their views will be properly taken account of in the development process. An essential facet of the champion's role is to promote teamworking amongst those involved, many of whom will come from very different cultural backgrounds. The champion should therefore be able to demonstrate an ability to work collaboratively with a number of different types of organizations. An individual with a single sector background is unlikely to be a successful champion.

Business planning skills

The champion's key output is the production of a partnership development strategy (or delivery contract in the case of a commercially based partnership). Every PPP's development strategy or contract will be different, as will be the level of detail required, but it is likely to contain the following elements:

- a summary of the PPP's overall objectives. These should be fairly clear from the earlier initial discussion phase but will need to be clarified in a form that can be used in the detailed negotiations with potential partners and ultimately approved by the partnership;

- proposals in respect of structural issues (such as membership, the role of the chair, organizational structure, the role of any director/secretariat, legal options and so on);

- proposals in respect of resourcing issues;

- suggested targets, success criteria, and impacts;

- a communications strategy to establish and maintain ongoing commitment to the PPP.

These latter elements will be considered in later chapters.

It is important to note that, while structural issues will form an important element of the partnership development strategy, they should not dominate the strategy; bureaucratic organizations love to discuss structures and tend to lose sight of overall objectives and success criteria. The private sector, on the other hand, is much more comfortable working on a 'management by objectives' basis and is generally more relaxed about structures. The champion will have to demonstrate the necessary political skills to ensure that the partnership development strategy represents a properly holistic approach and is not likely to become a hostage to subsequent structural discussions. The range and scale of business planning skills needed by a particular partnership champion will clearly vary from PPP to PPP according to circumstances.

INTERIM ORGANIZATIONAL STRUCTURE

The process for actually identifying a partnership champion (or project manager) will be different in every case. However it is useful to adopt some general guidelines to help the process.

The preliminary stages of the partnership lifecycle (as per Figure 2.1) will need to be guided in a way which is acceptable to all the partnership drivers. As noted above, initially there is likely to be a fairly small group of officers or enthusiasts working on an informal basis. However there will come a time when this group will need to evolve into a more formal steering group of some sort; ideally there should be as few rules as possible governing the composition and terms of reference of such a group – the key is to bring together those individuals who are keen to establish the partnership (regardless of their background and status within their own organization); enthusiasm and clarity of vision are the watchwords. It is worth considering the inclusion of a few local heavyweight individuals (in a political sense; this is particularly important in councils developing service delivery partnerships) at this stage if the steering group is to have local credibility; the group should also include sufficient officers who will understand and be able to advise on the detailed functional requirements of a successful PPP. It is, however, a policy development exercise rather than a management task and the personal skills of the steering group need to recognize this bias. Perhaps the only rule is that the members of the steering group must recognize that their's is a temporary role to oversee the preliminary stages (just as the partnership champion's position is temporary). The object of the exercise is to deliver a partnership development strategy or service delivery contract which is acceptable to the partners.

The steering group will need to elect from amongst their members a chairperson with sufficient status to have the respect of all the key drivers; it is important that the chair is not the partnership champion since the latter (who will be doing all the detailed work in the preliminary stages) will need to be responsible to someone. This is essential if the process is to be able to demonstrate accountability to the wider stakeholder group. In the case of a commercially based partnership, once a preferred bidder has been identified, it is sometimes sensible to have joint chairs of the steering group to help emphasize the partnership nature of the process. The role of chair of the steering group is of equal importance to that of the champion to the success of this stage in the process. While the champion will be undertaking the detailed work the chair will be the public face of the process and may well have to take the lead in negotiating with potential partners. It is important therefore that, just as with the choice of champion, care is taken over selecting the chair; 'Buggins turn' is not an option. The traditional solution in the UK is to allow the chair to emerge following informal consultation. This has been a surprisingly effective approach but can be viewed as being out of step with the modern world – an important consideration given that the PPP movement is trying to attract new types of partners and operate in a new way. There is no correct way of appointing a chair for the steering group since circumstances will differ for every partnership; all that can be done is to encourage openness and inclusiveness in the process.

CASE STUDIES: The partnership development process – steering groups and champions

Inevitably the key drivers of statutory based partnerships are likely to be from the relevant public body although most organizations involve likely partners fairly early in the process – for example the *Hastings Local Strategic Partnership* was initially discussed by members and officials from the health sector, the voluntary sector and the chamber of commerce working with the local authority. This pattern appears to have been repeated elsewhere with the partnership champion role filled by an appropriate local authority officer. The key drivers in voluntary based partnerships are more diverse although again local authorities seem to be the most proactive. The process to establish the *Bedfordshire and Luton Economic Development Partnership* was driven by a steering group of economic development officers for the local authorities in the area working with the chamber of commerce; however there was no formal chair with the driving energy coming from within the group. *Hampshire* adopted a slightly different approach when establishing its economic partnership: the county council, having identified a need for a partnership, invited a retired business man to take the lead and he did this by involving the key business leaders from the various industrial sectors in the county. The council provided the secretariat during this development phase. The early stages of a service delivery partnership inevitably has to be driven by the tendering authority but three important features appear to be necessary for success – members need to be involved as well as officers, there needs to be a coherent communication strategy and it is essential that there is a nominated officer in charge of the process. All three features are mentioned in their review of strategic service delivery partnerships by the New Local Government Network and can, for example, be seen in the way that both *Middlesbrough* and *Milton Keynes* councils ran their respective tendering process for their support services.

While the appointment of the chair is necessarily a fairly opaque process the appointment of the partnership champion, particularly for voluntary based partnerships but also for some statutory based partnerships, needs to be as open as possible. The champion will, however, have to work closely with the chair and the relationship between the two is crucial to the success of the preliminary stages. It is however important that others are involved in the selection process for the champion – the latter must enjoy the confidence of all the potential partners if the PPP is to be launched successfully. The chair will need to be sensitive as to whom to invite to join the selection process – the inevitable tendency to invite representation from all the potential partners (the inclusivity argument) has to be balanced with the need for effectiveness.

Before seeking candidates for the post of partnership champion the steering group will need to define a fairly clear job specification, a person specification, a remuneration package (if one is to be offered – frequently the post can be filled on a seconded basis with the employer organization happy to contribute the cost as part of their support for the PPP) and the expected time commitment. It is important that the steering group as a whole clarifies these points at the outset and does not just leave it to the chair – any misunderstandings at this stage can make it very difficult for the champion, once appointed, to carry out their role effectively.

Given that one of the key skills required of the champion will be local knowledge (whether geographic or subject), candidates for the post are likely to come from two possible sources:

- they may already be employees of one of the potential partner organizations;
- they may have particularly relevant personal expertise but be working in an organization which is unlikely to become involved in the PPP.

The first group of candidates are fairly easy to reach by circulating information through the existing structures of potential partners; the second group is more difficult. While word of mouth is the easiest, this approach is open to the charge of exclusivity; some steering groups therefore advertise locally as well. This combines the advantage of possibly attracting a good candidate with that of publicizing the PPP proposal. The choice of a champion (or project manager) for commercially based PPPs is generally more straightforward since the candidates are likely to come from the contracting parties; the individual chosen must, however, have the confidence of all the principal partners.

SUMMARY

- Understand the PPP lifecycle; ensure that adequate time is spent on the preliminary stages in order to ensure that all the potential partners and stakeholders understand the implications of establishing a partnership.

- Ensure there is clarity over why the PPP is needed, and what benefits it will offer to the potential partners.

- Apply logic to the identification of the key PPP drivers and work at ensuring their commitment from the start.

- Appreciate that, while the initial stages of a PPP's development may require confidentiality, openness and inclusivity should be introduced into every part of the process as soon as possible.

- Recognize the importance of a partnership champion or project manager, and develop clarity over the role and reporting framework.

- Establish a steering group of enthusiasts with a respected chair; again, develop clarity in their role.

- Recognize that the chair should not be the same individual as the champion in order to ensure a balanced and accountable approach to the strategy development process.

- Appreciate that neither the steering group nor the champion will necessarily feature in the long term structure (although the chair might do).

- Adopt a holistic approach to the partnership development strategy and ensure that structural discussions do not dominate.

CHAPTER 3

Partnership Development Strategy: Characteristics of Possible Partners

The previous chapter outlined the initial steps to be taken in developing a PPP – these steps will be common to all types of partnership, although the time frame will vary according to the nature of the partnership. As a result of these steps there should be a steering group of some sort, chaired by an individual acceptable to all the potential partners, and led by a partnership champion (or project manager) working with the chair. This group of stakeholders has the task of turning the initial ideas into reality. For commercially based partnerships the process of turning initial ideas into reality is a contractual development process which has to follow established contract definition and tendering steps. This is very different from the process undertaken for other types of partnerships and, because of this difference, is not covered in this book; a number of guidance notes covering the contract development process are however published by various organizations such as government agencies or local government bodies. Some of the comments in this chapter may nevertheless be of value to those involved in commercially based partnerships.

The first key task of the steering group for statutory or voluntary based partnerships is to firm up the inaugural membership of the PPP, and to gain their commitment. In parallel with this exercise, governance and resourcing principles will need to be developed; these are discussed in the following chapters but, in practice, the degree of potential partners' commitment will depend upon their support for the governance and resourcing issues. The twin-track nature of this process has inevitable dangers and the success of the process will depend to a large extent upon the skills of the chair and champion working together, and their understanding of the political aspirations of the potential partners.

In approaching potential partners the fundamental selling point which the chair and champion must continue to emphasize is the benefit which the PPP will bring to the partner's own functions. This added value has to be seen as being worth more than any drawbacks (either political or resource) which the potential partners might perceive. It follows that the chair and champion need to develop a close understanding of the objectives, decision-making structure and resource constraints of each partner; these will inevitably be different in each case which means that a different partnership engagement strategy will need to be adopted for each potential partner. A second issue which the steering group will need to consider at the outset is how to achieve a balanced membership of the PPP. Circumstances will differ but if it is to be successful, a PPP must demonstrate a genuine balance between different sectors, and must not be seen as merely an extension of one particular sector (such as the local authority). Potential partners must be assured that they are not there just to make up the numbers: they must feel that their sector will be able to make a positive contribution to the work of the PPP.

KEY SECTORS – APPROPRIATE APPROACHES

The following notes summarize some of the characteristics of potential partners which will need considering by the chair and champion when developing an appropriate negotiation strategy.

CENTRAL GOVERNMENT DEPARTMENTS AND AGENCIES

In many cases central government will not be relevant to the development of a PPP since, by their nature, PPPs are generally concerned with local or sub-regional issues. However central government does have a role to play in most statutory based PPPs, either directly or through the relevant regional agency; central government will also have a role to play in commercially based PPPs delivering a national policy or project. Where they are involved, central government departments are likely to have three particular interests:

- a *general* interest in promoting cross-sector collaboration. Government policy is to work in partnership and ministers like to claim that in support of this policy their department is working closely with a wide range of organizations;

- a *specific* interest in a PPP's outcomes insofar as they help meet particular national targets. For example, ministers will wish to quote specific crime reduction or health improvement figures achieved by relevant locally based PPPs.

- where a department has provided funding, a *financial* interest. Their interest in PFI-based contracts is self-evident; in many other cases government will have provided funding on a matched basis (for example specific community or educational projects). In these latter cases ministers will be interested in demonstrating the value of their department's contribution in levering in additional resources to deliver a particular policy.

Central departments are unlikely to be interested in how a PPP is managed or the details of its activities; they will only really be interested in outcomes and how they can be used to demonstrate the success of government policy. It is therefore unlikely that a government department will wish to be directly involved as a partner in a PPP except perhaps where a major PFI scheme is being managed through a PPP. Having said that, however, it may well be useful for the chair or champion of a PPP which might have relevance to a government department to keep that department informed of progress on an informal basis; departments do not like surprises so the development of informal contacts during the partnership development strategy process may well pay dividends later on. This is particularly true if, as a result of a PPP's actions, a subsequent bid for funding is submitted by one of the partners (or the PPP itself) – for example a proposal to develop a facility such as a community-based university may come forward as a result of a local regeneration strategy; such a facility would require extra funding from government via the University Funding Council. The Council (and Department for Education and Skills) would appreciate the earliest possible warning of such a request.

REGIONAL AGENCIES

The development of regional agencies has been a major feature of the constitutional landscape of the UK over the last ten years or so (and also elsewhere in Europe although to a lesser extent since continental Europe embraced regionalism earlier than the UK). While the UK landscape is continuing to evolve, Scotland and Wales now have their own devolved structure (each with slightly different powers) but the position in England is still developing. The regional Government Offices (GOs) and the Regional Development Agencies (RDAs) now have significant resources, as do the two executive bodies in Scotland and Wales. At this stage in their development Regional Assemblies in England have limited resources of their own although they are growing in influence. A number of other organizations, such as the NHS or Housing Corporation, also operate on a regional basis; while maintaining links with GOs and RDAs they remain very autonomous reporting through their own national structures (unlike the Small Business Service and the Learning and Skills Council – see below). The resources available to regional agencies are often channelled through PPPs or spent on the advice of local PPPs.

This is a somewhat confused picture and it is hardly surprising that, at this relatively early stage in the development of regionalism in the UK, there remains a certain amount of tension in the motivation of the various regional agencies (particularly in England). At one extreme, regional bodies see themselves as representing central government and promoting central policy; at the other extreme, they see themselves as representing the interests of their region and the local bodies within the region. This inevitably places them in a somewhat ambiguous position vis-à-vis locally based PPPs. Where the regional agencies are providing resources to a PPP they will then have to decide whether they are regulating the consequences (in which case they can hardly be a partner), or whether they are part of the delivery process (in which case they can reasonably expect to become a partner). Even if they are not providing resources and are only using a PPP in an advisory capacity, regional agencies are likely to be important stakeholders in most PPPs (even in commercially driven PPPs).

While the relationship between each PPP and the appropriate regional body will depend upon circumstances it is important that the chair and champion consider this relationship very carefully at the outset. The regional bodies will already have directly established links with relevant local bodies who are likely to become partners in a PPP (for example the regional GO will have a link with the local authority, the regional office of the NHS will have a direct link with the local health trusts, and the RDA will have a link with local business, probably via the chamber of commerce). Any links developed between a PPP and the regional bodies will have to take account of the existing bilateral links and cannot be allowed to damage those individual relationships; hence the need for careful consideration at the outset.

Generally speaking regional agencies have adopted structures under which specific individuals at regional level take responsibility for particular local areas – for example the GO for the South East (GOSE) has a director responsible for the Kent area, together with a supporting team of specialists. These directors, or team leaders, will be the key contact point for the PPP chair and champion. A practical solution which is often acceptable to a regional agency is to keep them advised of a PPP's activities by including them in the circulation of papers and inviting them to attend meetings as appropriate. The alternative of making a regional agency a full member of a PPP has the potential conflict of interest drawbacks, as noted above, of which the steering group needs to be aware.

SMALL BUSINESS SERVICE (SBS) AND LEARNING AND SKILLS COUNCIL (LSC)

These two organizations merit a section of their own because they are, in many ways, hybrid organizations (although their current status may change as a result of national policy). Although they are national organizations with their own national councils they operate through local structures which are coordinated at a regional level. They are increasingly being required to work with and through the RDAs and, to some extent, GOs. Ultimately they are judged on their achievement of national targets but these are achieved through local delivery mechanisms (subcontracted in the case of the SBS). Both organizations have significant resources and they are likely to be of considerable importance to the work of both PPPs and the individual partners within PPPs – for example the LSC funds the further education sector. However the structure of both may well change over the next few years with the regional dimension becoming more important. Their hybrid nature has meant that there is no coherent relationship between themselves and PPPs; for example 73 per cent of Local Strategic Partnerships include the local LSC as members but only 5 per cent have the SBS as a member (2002 Survey: Table 8). Most economic partnerships appear to have involved both organizations while all learning partnerships seem to have included the LSC (their principal funder).

The relationship between PPPs and the two organizations is likely to evolve over the next few years; from a PPP point of view the important thing will be to ensure that if it is decided to include them, such inclusion will not detrimentally affect the participation of local organizations (such as colleges or the chamber of commerce) in the work of the partnership.

LOCAL AUTHORITIES

Local authorities, by their very nature and breadth of responsibilities, will almost certainly be key members of all PPPs. Indeed Part 1 of the 2000 Local Government Act places a general obligation on local authorities to promote the overall welfare of their community, and to coordinate the production of a local community strategy. However local authorities are unusual bodies. Councillors are elected for fairly short periods; their interests are almost always local, sometimes even parochial, and they are keen to exercise direct control over most issues. The degree of freedom accorded to officers varies widely but it is the officers who understand the intricacies of the rules under which authorities work and who play a key role in determining the agenda and business management process. It is often the officers who will serve on a PPP's initial steering group although some authorities will insist on a councillor also being present. The modus operandi of each council will be different but it is essential that the chair and champion of the PPP fully understand the local council dynamics if the latter's commitment is to be obtained.

In many ways local authorities are likely to be the primary beneficiary of a PPP. Chapter 2 outlined the principal reasons for establishing a PPP and it can be seen that local authorities are direct beneficiaries from all of these; in particular PPPs represent a key way for local authorities to demonstrate accountability to, and the involvement of, the local community. PPPs (particularly contractually based partnerships delivering local services) also represent an extremely effective way of levering in additional resources in support of their policies; this is particularly attractive to officers who are constantly being required to operate with less resource. However the very fact that local authorities are the principal beneficiaries of PPPs means that they also have the potential to lose the most. Local politicians are elected to deliver local results and it is not always in their re-election interests to have to share the benefits of a PPP's activities with other partners. There is therefore an inevitable tension between the motivation of councillors and officers when the council becomes involved in a PPP. There is also potential tension between different departments of a council when the authority enters into a contract with a private sector contractor or consortium to deliver services under the auspices of a partnership; the impact on both staffing and quality of services will differ amongst the council's various departments. There are therefore a number of potential conflicts of opinion and approach within a local authority, regardless of whether or not the council has a policy to work in partnership with others.

Teasing out and understanding these tensions at the outset is a key task of the chair and champion. A two-pronged approach is often the most successful one, with the chair (who could be a councillor) taking on the role of negotiating with and winning over the elected members while the PPP champion works through the relevant officers. Whatever approach is adopted, however, it is essential that it is coordinated and that both levels of the council are committed to the PPP.

THE HEALTH COMMUNITY

The health community, along with the education sector, has been obliged by the government to be pioneers in the use of PFI-based partnerships; they have therefore developed their own structures to participate in this initiative. In addition the scope of the health community to contribute to wider goals is becoming increasingly recognized. While the direct relationship between the health of a community to issues such as housing and education has long been recognized, it needs to be remembered that the health sector is the largest employer in the UK. Thus the health sector is extremely interested in economic development. Up until recently it has been difficult to engage the health community in any joint sector initiatives, mainly because the health sector itself has been so fractious in its structure while, at the same time, grappling with the consequences of procurement through PFI. The creation of Primary Care Trusts (of which there are now 302 covering the whole of England) should, however, considerably simplify matters. These trusts, with responsibility for articulating a comprehensive health strategy for the community, and for purchasing services to deliver the strategy, can contribute a coherent health view to a PPP whether the partnership's interest is in education, housing, or economic development.

The health community is unlikely to contribute significant resources to a PPP unless it is statutorily obliged to do so (such as to a local Health Forum) since its resources are so closely tied by central government to the achievement of specific targets. On the other hand the health community can contribute significant expertize and valuable statistics (which they are required to keep by government in any case) to the work of a PPP.

The process for engaging the health community is likely to be very similar to that for a local authority. There will be an appointed trust board to which the officers are responsible; that board is likely to include local authority representatives. In the initial stages of a PPP's development it is often appropriate for the steering group's chair to approach a relevant trust board member while the champion has more detailed discussions with the appropriate officers.

THE EDUCATION SECTOR

The education sector is much more diverse than health; although the sector as a whole will be interested in community development, and will therefore wish to become involved in bodies such as LSPs, there will be differences in the interests of the various educational levels. For example at the primary level the sector will be more interested in community-oriented PPPs, while at the secondary or higher/further level the sector's interest will be more likely to be in economic development or possibly housing. The HE/FE sector may also be interested in developing additional specific services for the community through a commercially based PPP.

In most parts of the UK there is very limited coordination of the education sector – while the local authority has certain statutory duties these do not cover the private education sector, and only impinge in a fairly peripheral way on the HE/FE sectors. This is starting to change with the creation of different versions of Lifelong Learning Partnerships (LLP) (which themselves are of course PPPs) but the lifelong learning movement is still in its infancy; a particular problem is how to attract the private sector given that most LLPs try to accommodate the full range of educational interests. This inevitably means that an LLP tends to be supplier dominated, which is an unattractive proposition for the private sector.

Given the current development stage of the LLP movement, there appear to be three possible ways of involving the education sector in wider strategically oriented PPPs. The first is to involve a local 'umbrella' body such as the Learning and Skills Council (LSC); however as noted above (SBS and LSC section), this approach suffers from the fundamental difficulty that the LSC is often the principal funder of many of the local institutions and is not directly connected to all. This means that the individual institutions are reluctant to allow the LSC to speak for them. A local authority education department suffers from the same drawback. The second alternative is to invite a specific educational body (such as a university) to become a member of the PPP but this runs the risk of alienating the other institutions in the sector (unless only one institution has the specific strengths needed for the PPP in question). The third approach is to try to involve a collectively representative body (such as a local HE/FE coordinating group, or a secondary schools strategy group) but this assumes that whatever collective body is invited will be able to secure the commitment of its members to the PPP.

Partnerships devoted to delivering specific services however are likely to be able to attract those educational institutions with a direct interest in the relevant services. It is apparent that gaining the support and commitment of the education sector is difficult and much will depend on local circumstances.

THE VOLUNTARY AND COMMUNITY SECTOR

There is a very similar challenge in how to generate support from the local voluntary and community sector in PPPs. There is little cohesion in this sector despite the work of such bodies as local Councils for Voluntary Organizations (CVOs). This is hardly surprising given that most voluntary groups tend to focus on particular topics or issues; that is, after all, why they have been established. They are also, in general, reluctant to give up their independence in any way and tend to rely on the dedication of a relatively small group of enthusiastic individuals. There are some exceptions to this – for example organizations such as Age Concern cover a wide range of issues as they affect their particular constituency and are generally well structured and reasonably resourced; national charities are also often sufficiently well resourced to contribute to a PPP and may therefore wish to expand their range of services through a dedicated service delivery partnership.

This contextual situation makes it difficult to involve the local voluntary and community sector in a statutory or voluntary based PPP despite the fact that their input is often envisaged as extremely important – for example PPPs involved in housing, health or community development need to be working with relevant community groups if they are to be successful.

There can be no firm guidelines on how to involve the local voluntary and community sector in PPPs since the relative strength and spread of community organisations will vary from place to place. The PPP chair and champion, working with the steering group, will need to identify the relevant local groups and assess their robustness and quality of leadership; this process will be greatly helped if there is an active local umbrella organization of some sort. They need, however, to be aware of the danger of involving 'the usual suspects'.

THE PRIVATE SECTOR

Almost every government partnership initiative stresses the importance of involving the private sector. But unfortunately the private sector is not a single coherent group. It consists of a large number of individual businesses, some 80 per cent of which employ fewer than 20 staff. These small businesses are unlikely to want (or be able) to commit scarce resources to partnership working unless there is a direct benefit to them; many of them belong to chambers of commerce to keep in touch. Equally many of the larger businesses will have no real interest in partnership working – they are too busy trying to survive in an increasingly competitive world. This makes the problem of engaging the private sector very difficult, particularly in statutory or voluntary PPPs (where participation will tend to be based on civic duty or altruism); the position is very different for commercially based PPPs with their more specific benefits for the sector. It is therefore difficult to engage individual businesses in a statutory or voluntary PPP process, particularly at the outset (the position changes once a PPP can demonstrate a track record and a company becomes concerned that it may be missing out in some way). It is primarily for this reason that discussions on the establishment of such PPPs generally involve the local chamber of commerce (or their equivalent – in some parts of the UK the chamber of trade or trade associations may be more relevant); not only are they able to provide partnership development resources but they should also have strong links with individual companies (who will only join chambers if they see advantages in developing networks and working together).

Working with chambers does, however, have two particular drawbacks. First chambers' own un-earmarked resources are limited; their subscription income is essentially to provide services for their members rather than to subsidize the development of community activities such as PPPs. Secondly there is a danger that a chamber will view the PPP development process as an end in itself (fulfilling its 'local charter') rather than as a way of promoting genuine involvement from individual members. It is the latter group, with their more unlimited resources, enthusiasm and skills with which PPPs needs to engage in the longer term. Nevertheless the involvement of the local chamber is essential in the short term if a statutory or voluntary based PPP is to develop a coherent strategy which will attract the support of the private sector. As with some of the constituencies mentioned above a two-pronged approach is often the most successful, with the chair handling discussions with chamber board members and the champion dealing with appropriate officers.

It should also be noted that some major corporate players choose not to belong to the local chamber; they may however be particularly keen to contribute to the development of local initiatives. The position will vary from area to area, which once again demonstrates the need to ensure that the chair and champion have excellent local contacts.

Commercially based PPPs (particularly PFI partnerships) are very different as far as the private sector is concerned – individual companies are the key players in this process and will develop their own organizational structures to enable them to play their part. They are often the initiators of such partnerships and devote considerable resources to the process; however it is important that they are not perceived as driving the partnership development process from a purely commercial (profit) point of view; long-term success will only come from demonstrating partnership thinking.

DEVELOPING A STAKEHOLDER MAP

The previous notes summarized the key sectors which are likely to be involved in the strategy development process, and suggested how they might be approached. But not all the sectors will be relevant and care needs to be taken at the outset to ensure that time and resources are not wasted unnecessarily. There needs to be a logical way of planning the approach to potential partners, and one of the most effective ways of doing so is to develop a stakeholder map before starting any detailed discussions with possible partners. This process should be undertaken by the champion working with the chair and through the steering group. The purpose of a stakeholder map is to provide a logical framework to guide the membership negotiations with potential partners. In order to do this an assessment needs to be made under three criteria – first, how will the proposed PPP benefit the potential partner; this requires an understanding of both the aims of the PPP and the objectives of the partner and how they match. Secondly, what will the cost be to the partner if they join the PPP; this has to be based on a realistic assessment of the PPP's costs, how those costs might be met, and an appreciation of the partner's own financial position and systems. And thirdly, how important will the membership of a particular partner be to the success of the PPP. The combination of these three criteria will then guide the negotiating strategy with each potential partner.

In developing a stakeholder map a few principles are worth bearing in mind:

- Avoid plotting too many potential stakeholders and thus over-complicating the whole process. The aim at this stage is to engage the key organizations and individuals; others can be encouraged to join later.

- Be realistic in the assessment of the likely time and level of commitment to be sought from a potential partner. There is little point in entering long drawn out negotiations with an organization which, in the end, will make a fairly limited contribution.

- Be prepared to subdivide within the individual partners, both in an organizational and individual sense – for example there will be various different possible contact points with a local authority. The aim is to produce a practical partnership development strategy, not a beautifully balanced but impossibly complex one.

There are various ways to develop a stakeholder map; at its very simplest the map will consist of a list of potential stakeholders with a few notes annotated against each one. A slightly more sophisticated approach is to attempt to quantify the three criteria listed above and thus produce a ranking of potential partners (which can be useful in determining a negotiation action plan). Figure 3.1 gives an example of this approach (using the development of a voluntary PPP to cover economic development).

A Possible stakeholders	B Potential benefit of PPP (where 0 = no benefit, 10 = maximum benefit)	C Potential cost of PPP (where 0 = no cost, 10 = maximum cost)	D Net benefit (i.e. B – C)	E Importance of stakeholder to PPP (where 0 = no importance, 10 = very important)	F Overall assessment (i.e. D + E)
Local Authority	• improved economy • increased revenue to L.A. • increased resource to function • increased involvement with private sector Value, say, 7	• officer time • no additional resources • sharing of influence Value, say, 2	Say, 5	Say, 7	12
Chamber of Commerce	• improved economy • increased subscriptions to chamber • increased involvement and influence Value, say, 8	• officer time • contribution of other resources Value, say, 3	Say, 5	Say, 8	13
Health sector	• improved economy (equals less demand for health) • involvement in business decisions Value, say, 6	• tightening of employment scene • officer time Value, say, 4	Say, 2	Say, 6	8
Education sector	• improved job prospects • involvement in business decisions and vice versa Value, say 7	• officer time • possible curriculum changes Value, say, 5	Say, 2	Say, 7	9
Voluntary sector	• improved economy • increased business support • involvement in business decisions Value, say, 4	• officer time (which they can ill afford) Value, say, 3	Say, 1	Say, 4	5

Figure 3.1   A possible stakeholder map for developing a PPP on economic development

This analysis, which can be carried down to a lower level to cover individuals or specific departments, suggests that it is essential for the private sector and the local authority to be involved, useful for the education and health sectors, but of limited value for the voluntary sector. Column D (Net benefit of the PPP) will help frame the approach to the partner while Column E (Importance to the PPP) is useful in determining how much time and effort the chair/champion should expend on the potential partner in question. While the values given to the various headings can be disputed the methodology outlined in Figure 3.1 can be applied to any PPP proposal. It is also useful if, as part of the development of a stakeholder map, the individual contacts in each of the stakeholders, and their strengths, weaknesses and value to the PPP development process, are identified; this will be of considerable help to the chair and champion in their subsequent discussions. This can only be done if either (or preferably both) of the chair and champion has good local political knowledge.

The development of a stakeholder map is a valuable tool when considering potential partners in statutory or voluntary based PPPs and may be of some use for some commercially based PPPs, particularly in the identification of which individual departments or sections within the public sector body should be involved. At the micro level the approach can be adopted to help in the identification of particular individuals. The essential value of a stakeholder map is that it provides a logical framework to help guide the negotiations with potential partners; it is important that the latter process is not carried out in an ad hoc manner since to do so runs the risk of alienating some organizations through a rushed or ill-thought-through approach.

NEGOTIATION PROCESS

Once a stakeholder map has been prepared the next step is to develop a strategy on how to approach each stakeholder; the general principles to guide this process are:

- Ensure that there is a clear allocation of responsibility – who is going to approach whom. While most of the work will be done by the chair or champion there may be particular instances where a member of the steering group might be more appropriate. The most important thing is to ensure that potential partners are not confused by being approached by different people emphasising different aspects of the PPP proposal.

- Ensure that whoever takes the lead with a particular potential stakeholder has a clear understanding of that stakeholder's aims, organizational structure and culture.

- Ensure that negotiations are conducted on the basis of a common proposition in terms of the PPP's aims, its benefits to potential partners, its possible organizational structure and resource implications. While details will clearly change as individual negotiations proceed, agreement on the main principles needs to be obtained from the start to avoid later misunderstandings.

It is important that the strategy for handling negotiations with individual stakeholders is discussed and agreed with the steering group because there is a danger that individual members of the group (who are there, in general, because of their personal enthusiasm) may inadvertently misrepresent the case for the PPP in the course of their day-to-day activities. In particular there is a danger that semi-developed ideas over possible structures and resourcing issues may prejudice a subsequent, more formal, approach to potential partners. Whatever category of PPP is envisaged it is therefore useful to adhere to the following stages:

1. Clarification of the PPP's aims and objectives by the steering group. The initial ideas need to be developed as far as possible before wider dissemination.

2. Development of a stakeholder map of some sort. The map must be comprehensive and realistic. The exercise should be undertaken by the PPP champion working with the chair, and highlights the importance of ensuring that, between them, they have the necessary local knowledge.

3. Agreement on the principles to underpin the proposed organizational structure and resource model for the PPP; options on these aspects are considered in greater detail in the following chapters but it is important that steering group members are comfortable with the overall shape of what is proposed.

4. Identification of the key individuals to be approached in each potential partner (to be derived from the stakeholder mapping exercise).

5. Agreement on how each approach is to be handled. One practical point to be considered at this stage is timescale – most organizations likely to be involved in a PPP have a regular schedule of meetings and a timescale must be constructed which does not create potential conflicts between partners; for example councillors are often board members of local health trusts, college governors or members of chamber boards. It is important that they do not unduly influence (either positively or negatively) the decision of potential partners through prior knowledge.

Above all the key is to ensure that the process of approaching potential partners is well thought out and backed by a clear prospectus; inevitably this takes time and must not be rushed. While the retention of flexibility, particularly over final structure and resources, is desirable, uncoordinated ad hocery is to be avoided. A mistake made at this stage can be extremely costly – indeed it could be fatal to the process of trying to establish a partnership.

SUMMARY

- It is essential to get off to a good start in recruiting partners to a PPP – the aim is to build confidence and commitment from the outset.

- The negotiating process should be led by the chair and champion with the full support of the steering group.

- The identification of potential partners should be based on logical analysis and a realistic assessment of both the advantages which the PPP will bring them and the benefits which they will bring to the PPP.

- The steering group needs to endorse a clear statement on the aims and objectives of the PPP and have a clear idea of possible structures and resourcing of the PPP before any approaches are made to potential partners.

- In developing their detailed approach to potential partners the chair and champion should analyse the objectives, cultural approach, and existing organizational links of each partner; the PPP proposal must not be seen as a possible threat to the existing status quo but as a real benefit that will strengthen a partner.

- Clarity of the roles of the individuals involved in the negotiating process is vitally important in order to avoid creating confusion in the mind of potential partners.

- Like all negotiating processes success will depend on the interpersonal skills of the chair and champion and their ability to sell what could be seen as a complex (and possibly threatening) proposal in a straightforward way.

- Take time over the whole identification and negotiation process – it cannot be rushed.

CHAPTER 4

Partnership Development Strategy: Organizational Structure

The previous two chapters have discussed the initial steps to be taken in setting up a PPP; the next two chapters go on to consider the organizational and resourcing issues which also need to be addressed at the outset. While these issues are generically similar for all types of partnership their specific application will depend on the precise nature of each PPP. For example statutory based partnerships will have many of its operational requirements set out in the relevant legislation (for example the role of the local police commander in a Crime and Community Safety Partnership is specified); for other types of PPP however there is much greater freedom in how they are organized. The partners in a commercially based partnership will, for example, agree on the appropriate organizational structure as part of the contracting process.

The nature of public organizations means that, in general, they have a tendency to try and finalize organizational and resourcing issues as part of the preliminary discussion process. They do not really like to proceed by agreeing to something in principle and then considering the details later; they prefer to be clear from the outset on the complete package. This inevitably restricts the negotiating position of their representatives in the initial stages of the establishment of a PPP (which, because it is a new type of organization, will inevitably raise a number of precedents). All those involved in the negotiation process will be feeling their way since each potential partner will wish to influence the way the PPP is set up as part of their consideration of whether or not they wish to join. The chair and champion will therefore be working with a constantly changing canvass, a situation which re-emphasizes the importance of the need for these individuals to have excellent interpersonal and communication skills; it also illustrates the importance of the two working closely together.

It is also worth recognizing that because of the different nature of a PPP the organizational discussions with potential partners cannot be based on a logical checklist approach. The process will be very disjointed, with different issues arising all the time. Each partner will have their own priorities (or even sacred cows) and will be looking to end up with a total package acceptable to their own stakeholders. Essentially the nature of the discussions will be similar to those which take place constantly in the European Union – each sovereign state approaches discussions on a particular issue with their own objectives and principles in mind, and will only compromise on one aspect if they can gain an advantage elsewhere. The process to establish the structure of a PPP is the same – for example the private sector may start by insisting that the chair of, say, a PPP concerned with skills or education should be an employer; they may, however, be prepared to accept an alternative nominee provided the employers are the largest single group on the board (as opposed to the educational or local authority sectors). There will be similar negotiations around the precise nature of a PPP board set up to deliver a PFI project or range of services – for example, what will be the balance of power on the partnership board and how will that affect the level of influence that the board will have over the day-to-day freedom of the contractor?

This does not mean that there should be no organizational parameters to the discussions with individual partners; the steering group needs to agree on the principles within which negotiations can take place. The chair and champion will also need guidance on how much freedom they can have in their discussions with potential partners. In this chapter the pros and cons of alternative structural options are considered while Chapter 5 looks at the more detailed aspects of a PPP's organization.

There are two extreme organizational models:

- an informal partnership with minimum structures, operating by consensus amongst the partners;

- a formal company structure, operating under the provisions of the Companies Act.

Between these two extremes are variations – for example the members of an informal partnership can agree to bind themselves formally to operate in certain ways, while a company's articles can be as broad or specific as the members wish.

AN INFORMAL PARTNERSHIP

The most informal partnership is one where representatives of the partners meet and discuss issues in a fairly wide-ranging manner unencumbered by detailed terms of reference or procedures; the steering group approach as outlined in Chapter 2 is an example of such a partnership. It can be flexible in membership, both numerically and as far as status is concerned. Generally speaking this means that individual representatives tend to speak on their own behalf without a specific mandate from their constituency and will be reluctant (or unable) to commit their organizations to any particular action without reference back. The appointment of a chair and the administration of the partnership's affairs can be agreed on an informal basis and the partnership is unlikely to have any resources of its own to carry out any executive action – it will have to rely on the goodwill of one of its members.

Such a structure is very useful at the outset of a project (such as one to consider whether or not to establish a PPP) and may also be useful when developing preliminary thoughts on a possible policy initiative. It is also a helpful way to bring together for the first time representatives from a range of different backgrounds since the lack of structure means that they will feel more inclined to speak their minds and explore different ways of working together without commitment. An informal partnership is therefore a very useful way of bringing together a wide range of individuals from disparate backgrounds. However such a structure is inherently weak and unlikely to deliver any significant developments or actions. In particular the lack of direct accountability of the members (in the sense that they will generally need to refer back to their constituency on any substantive points) means that the inevitably slow rate of progress will ultimately discourage the more action-oriented partners from participating. In effect it is a more process-oriented structure than an action-oriented one.

A FORMAL PARTNERSHIP

It is fairly easy to progress from an informal partnership to a more formal structure provided there is goodwill and support around the table. In this context the term formal partnership is taken to mean one with specific terms of reference and with a defined membership and procedures, although the degree of formality will vary from partnership to partnership; the method of recording the arrangement will also depend on local circumstances. A formal partnership of this nature does not have any legal status and cannot therefore enter into contractual commitments with a third party; a 'partnership company' can, of course, be formed but it then becomes a company structure subject to the Companies Act and, despite its name, is not a partnership in the sense of this section – see the following section. The simplest way of creating a formal partnership is to produce a 'partnership deed' or 'memorandum' of some sort which is signed by each partner; the provisions of such a deed could, by agreement, be enforceable by law but it is more usual to work on the assumption that all partners will comply voluntarily with the deed – going to law to enforce a partnership is essentially a contradiction in terms. An alternative to a partnership deed is to attach the same provisions to a set of minutes subsequently agreed by all the partner representatives. A PFI or service delivery PPP will often be a formal partnership set up to deliver the contract or services which can then be attached as an appendix to the partnership agreement. Most statutory based partnerships are formal partnerships with any delivery requirements carried out by one of the partners – for example 95 per cent of LSPs operate under varying degrees of formality with only 5 per cent adopting a legal company structure.

It is useful if the partnership deed (or similar) covers the following points:

- the overall objective of the PPP;
- the specific actions which the PPP will undertake to achieve that objective;
- the names of the partners or members;
- the composition and powers of the board;
- the process by which the chair will be appointed and their term of office;
- the arrangements for administering and resourcing the work of the PPP.

The degree of detail to be included will be a matter for each PPP; a good working rule is to be as brief as possible – stick to the principles and avoid introducing anything which will restrict the future development of the partnership. This principle can also apply to a commercially based partnership – the governance arrangements for the partnership itself can be brief while the contract (what the partnership delivers) will be a very detailed specification.

There is no theoretical reason why a formal partnership cannot be used as a vehicle for any type of PPP – if the members wish they can agree that one of the partners carries out any executive action required (including handling partnership resources or employing staff). Such a structure does, however, presume that all the partners are wholly confident in the ability of one of their co-partners to deliver. This is not always possible where there is volatility in the delivery partner's own funding arrangements. For example a health authority or trust might undertake to deliver certain services on behalf of a PPP but then be prevented from doing so by a directive from central government. It is mainly for this reason that many PPPs, particularly of a voluntary nature, while happy to start operating on a formal partnership basis, subsequently consider moving to a more independent legal structure.

COMPANY STRUCTURE

Companies, whether limited by guarantee or shares, are governed by the Companies Act which sets out the duties of directors and boards, reporting requirements and so on. Any company set up to carry out the work of a PPP can introduce its own specific requirements (for example the composition of the board and the voting structure can be specified to reflect partners' requirements) but such provisions will have to operate within the framework of the legislation.

A company structure is extremely useful where executive action or the common management of resources by the partnership itself is envisaged. It also demonstrates the independence and accountability of a PPP in a very obvious and formal basis – third parties deal with a legally separate body. It does, however, put a burden on partner representatives who become directors of the company. Representatives of public authorities are sometimes reluctant to take on the full legal responsibilities of a director as set out in the Companies Act (and which are becoming more onerous). Furthermore some public authorities like to rotate their nominations who therefore have limited time to become acquainted with their legal responsibilities – this can be uncomfortable and cause difficulties. Company legislation also obliges the partnership to hold formal AGMs, and prepare and submit accounts in a certain way, all of which have cost implications. In trading terms it also needs to be borne in mind that a PPP operating as a separate legal organization is unlikely to have a trading history or significant assets of its own (unless one or some of the partners agree to transfer assets, such as housing, to the new company). This lack of financial detail may make it difficult for third parties to agree to contract with the PPP company unless one of the partners agrees to act as a guarantor.

Despite these potential drawbacks an increasing number of voluntary partnerships are adopting a legal structure – for example all the economic partnerships in the South East now have such a structure, as does the voluntary partnership set up to promote the Oxford Cambridge Arc. Statutory partnerships are less likely to operate as a company although 5 per cent of LSPs do so (mainly those involved in the direct delivery of services under the Neighbourhood Renewal Programme). It is unlikely that a company would be the most appropriate structure for a commercially based PPP; the private sector contractor(s) undertaking the delivery process will already have their own legal structures and the role of the partnership will be advising and monitoring delivery – the partnership itself will not be trading.

Various types of company structures can be adopted for a PPP. The most common is a company limited by guarantee (rather than by shares) where the core partners become members with a limited liability of, say, £1 each. They are usually not-for-profit companies whose articles specify that no dividends to the members will be payable, that any surplus on the company's activities will be used to support and develop the company's objectives, and that any assets on winding up the company will be transferred to another organization with similar objectives (and not transferred to the members). Under present legislation this formula results in an exemption from Corporation Tax (other than tax due on surplus funds held temporarily in interest-bearing accounts). VAT is, however, subject to a different set of rules and frequently causes difficulties. Each case has to be looked at on its own merits, and is not made any easier by the apparently ad hoc way in which central and regional government agencies treat VAT when making grants to partnerships.

A point to bear in mind when establishing a company of this nature is the relevant legislation concerning local authorities. This legislation specifies that, if a local authority is perceived as having a 'material relationship' with a company (the definition of which is specified in terms of ownership and/or levels of trading activity), then that company may be deemed as a local authority company and therefore subject to certain financial restrictions. This may not matter but is both a potential constraint and a potential drawback to the non local authority partners – the last thing any private sector partner wants to see is a restriction on a partnership's activities or, in the final analysis, a transfer of a partnership's resources to the local authority. The existence of these legislative provisions is another reason why it is inadvisable to use a company structure for a commercially based PPP set up to deliver local authority services – a key advantage of delivering services on a contractual basis under the auspices of a partnership is the access which it gives to additional sources of finance available only to the private sector contractor.

There is therefore much to consider before deciding whether to adopt a company structure. The costs and consequential restrictions need to be weighed carefully against the benefits.

MAKING THE CHOICE

The steering group will need to have a fairly clear idea of which model they prefer before detailed discussions are opened with potential partners. In considering the options there are four related factors which need to be taken into account; these factors apply to all types of PPP:

1. Is the PPP to be merely a *discussion forum,* or is it to have an *executive role*? The more executive the role, the more need there will be for the adoption of a more formal structure. Within the two extremes of discussion or execution there are variations – for example the approval of a Crime and Community Safety Partnership is often required before some executive action is carried out by the local authority or police; thus the partnership, while not being executive in the traditional sense, has de facto executive power. A similar situation may exist in a commercially based PPP with the approval of the board being required before the contractor can deliver or amend a particular service. On the other hand a Local Strategic Partnership, which is also statutorily based, will generally have limited executive power other than to approve a local community plan and may not therefore need a formal voting structure. A voluntarily based economic or learning partnership could, with the agreement of its partners, undertake specific executive action (such as establishing and running an enterprise hub or equivalent agency) and will therefore need some way of ensuring formal agreement to a course of action.

2. Linked to this is the issue of *resources*. Is it envisaged that the PPP will have its own resources and that the partnership board will have freedom in how those resources can be used? In considering this it should be remembered that there are two basic categories of resource – the funds needed to administer or run the partnership, and the funds needed to deliver programmes coming under the auspices of the partnership. Again there are alternative options here – for example it could be agreed to meet a PPP's running costs via a subscription type approach and the subscriptions could be administered by one of the partners on behalf of the PPP; any programme funds could be handled directly by partners. A separate company would not be needed in that case. Alternatively the partners may be more comfortable with the subscription income being handled by a separate legal entity with programme funds handled either by individual partners or through the partnership company (or through both). In some PPP proposals partners may have the freedom to decide their preferred solution for managing resources but in other cases the solution may be determined by the relevant funding agency – for example housing corporation funds are routed through registered housing associations and are unlikely to be allocated directly to a PPP; however European funds are often available only to partnership bodies.

3. The third factor to be considered is that of *accountability*. How is it envisaged that the PPP will demonstrate accountability to its partners and/or to the community at large? If a very informal structure is adopted for a PPP it is sometimes difficult to assess its accountability – in an informal scenario board members do not always see it as part of their role to report back to their nominating body; regular annual reporting may tend to be overlooked. At the other end of the organizational spectrum the Companies Act places specific responsibilities on office holders and requires the publication of reports and accounts for shareholders. These might be regarded as being too onerous and the steering group will need to develop some guidelines on accountability before substantive discussions are held with potential partners. Chapter 7 considers the accountability issue in greater detail.

4. Alongside accountability is the need to demonstrate the *independence* of a PPP. A PPP exists to add value to the work of the individual partners and it can only do this by demonstrating to the partners that it is independent from any one partner. An informally structured PPP with poorly defined operational and accountability systems will inevitably be viewed with some suspicion by some partners. The greater the clarity of structure the better the perception of independence will be.

PPP option / Factors	Wholly informal	Formal with partnership deed	Company with limited powers	Company with full powers
Discussion only	X			
Authorisation body		X	X	
Executive			X	X
No resources	X	X		
Operating resources		X	X	X
Programme resources				X
All resources				X
Ad hoc accountability	X	X		
Formal accountability		X	X	X
Limited independence	X	X	X	
Full independence			X	X

Figure 4.1   Organizational options for a PPP

The requirements of every PPP will be different but the matrix in Figure 4.1 gives some guidance for developing the most appropriate structure for any PPP. In order to keep things simple the matrix uses only four organizational models but there can be subtle variations within and between each model. For example a company could be established with a small group of shareholders and board (who will therefore have specific legal responsibilities) but the articles could specify that certain aspects of their operations require the approval of a wider group of stakeholders. An example of this approach is the partnership company which has been established by a small number of the key stakeholders in Milton Keynes (who provide most of the running costs). The company itself undertakes no initiatives of its own but acts as the financial and legal contractor for programmes covering economic or learning developments approved by partnership boards which include a wider and more specialist range of stakeholders.

Before opening any discussions on structural options with potential partners the chair and champion will need to obtain the agreement of the steering group. This requires careful management to take account of the sensitivity of the issue; as mentioned earlier in this chapter there is a tendency to try and rush into final decisions on structure as early as possible (particularly if the individual members of the steering group become over-enthusiastic) but this should be resisted for two main reasons: first it is helpful to gain experience of how the PPP actually operates, and the support which it generates from the partners; and secondly the discussions with potential partners may reveal considerable differences in their approach to structure. There is also the

CASE STUDIES: Developing an appropriate organizational structure

Every PPP is different and they will develop their organizational structure to suit their own particular needs. While there is an increasing trend to establish their own legal identity some partnerships retain their informal status – for example the *Kent and Medway Economic Board*, with no executive delivery functions, remains an informal partnership with the county council employing the staff and undertaking any contractual commitments on behalf of the partnership. Both the *Hastings Local Strategic Partnership* and the *Bedfordshire and Luton Economic Development Partnership* are moving towards the establishment of a company limited by guarantee; the latter partnership is taking steps to ensure that the resultant company is not a local authority controlled organization in order not to restrict the partnership's freedom of action. In *Northamptonshire* the partnership is also creating a company structure but the county council is likely to remain the accountable body for the major projects funded by EMDA. The *Portsmouth and South East Hants Partnership*, which was originally established to bid for and manage SRB projects, has been a company for some years and has plans to build up its own independent portfolio of assets to support its other activities.

issue of cost – it is not worth spending a lot of money (and time) on developing complicated structures until there is a good measure of agreement amongst the potential partners.

Selling the 'make haste slowly' policy can be strengthened by pointing out to the steering group that the partnership's structure may well change as it becomes more established. A successful partnership may well take on more executive functions as the partners become more confident in its role. A number of PPPs start on a fairly informal basis and take some years to become more formally structured – the evolution of the economic partnerships in the South East is a good example of this. The eleven partnerships, which were all created on a voluntary basis covering a specific geographic area, were initially established on an informal basis over a period of about four or five years in the 1990s. Each was set up to meet their own locally perceived primary need, whether it was to promote inward investment (such as the Thames Valley Economic Partnership) or to promote specific economic initiatives (such as the Isle of Wight Partnership). The formation of the South East England Development Agency (SEEDA) and the Regional Assembly obliged them to become more formally structured and coordinated in their approach and, over time, all the partnerships have become legal entities with varying degrees of executive authority and range of responsibilities to suit their own local circumstances.

While the prospect of structural evolution over time may be fairly easy to justify and sell to the potential partners at the outset, there is one consequential issue which the steering group will need to address at this stage, which is 'how are subsequent changes going to be achieved?' Partnerships are established to achieve long-term objectives but circumstances change over time; they need therefore to adopt sustainable structures which can be adapted without negating the partnership's objectives. This simple issue is a potential minefield. Partnerships are launched on a wave of optimism and goodwill and it is tempting to assume that future organizational change can be achieved in the same way. But attitudes to a partnership may well change over time: the external context may change; the local political climate may change; relationships both with and within the private sector may change and so on. It is therefore dangerous to assume that the initial acceptance to future organizational change will continue forever; however it is equally dangerous to try and anticipate problems by seeking to tie the hands of the partners in the future (for example by specifying in the partnership deed or company articles that future structural change can be carried out by majority voting). This latter approach, while sensible in many ways, may prejudice the initial discussions – for example some of the partners may be very unwilling to bind their successors in this way and may only agree to a clause requiring 100 per cent agreement to any future organizational changes. While equally understandable (particularly from a local authority viewpoint) this may prevent any subsequent evolution of the partnership. A possible solution is to adopt a two tier approach whereby decisions on certain matters (such as core membership) require unanimity from the initial core members but on other matters (such as eligibility for the chairmanship) require only a majority.

This problem is only likely to arise with voluntary based partnerships since they have the greatest freedom of action and are the type of partnership which is most likely to become more executive in nature, thus requiring a change in organizational structure. Each PPP proposal will need to deal with this issue in their own way. In general terms a partnership can only really work if all the partners agree; it follows therefore that any agreement to allow future organizational change through majority voting may well be a hollow agreement in that, if a partner finds itself outvoted, it may just resign. While it may not be crucial to the future of, say, a housing partnership if a voluntary sector organization leaves because of a structural change of which they disapprove, it will undoubtedly affect the partnership's credibility. It will be for the chair and champion, as part of their initial negotiations with potential partners, to develop proposals which reassure them that future structural changes will be handled in an appropriately sensitive way.

SUMMARY

- While it is important that the steering group develop initial ideas on structure in order to guide the negotiations by the chair and champion with potential partners it is equally important to keep such ideas as fluid as possible for as long as possible.

- It is important to appreciate that potential partners will be looking at the overall package of what the proposed PPP will offer and cost; structure is only one element of the package.

- There are two extreme structural options – a wholly informal partnership or a formal company structure, with variations in between.

- The structure may well change as the PPP matures and partners become more confident in its work.

- The choice of structure will depend on a number of factors but a realistic option is to start on a fairly informal basis and only introduce more formality as required.

- Consideration will need to be given at the outset on how future structural changes should be handled.

CHAPTER 5

Partnership Development Strategy: Governance, Resources and Staffing

Once the steering group has developed their own ideas on the possible organizational structure, more detailed consideration can be given to specific issues; in particular the chair and champion will need to have some fairly clear ideas on the following areas when opening discussions with potential partners:

- the nature and role of the *members* of the partnership

- the nature and role of the *chair*

- the power and functions of the *board*

- the degree of *infrastructure* envisaged, and the nature of the post heading the infrastructure (such as an executive director)

- the *resourcing* of the partnership.

The previous chapter suggested that, as a PPP develops and partners become more confident in its activities, the basic organizational structure is likely to evolve into a more formal one; this is true across all categories of partnerships but is particularly true of voluntary based PPPs. The same evolutionary process may well happen in the areas covered in this chapter – the arrangements agreed at the outset can be regarded as the minimum baseline which is acceptable to all the partners at that point in time. As confidence grows and the partnership becomes established the baseline can be changed provided the partners agree – for example, membership can be extended or additional resources transferred to partnership control. It is therefore important that the initial arrangements are flexible enough to permit further development of the PPP in the future – this is just as true for partnerships based on statutory or contractual arrangements as for voluntary based partnerships.

MEMBERSHIP

Previous chapters suggested that most PPPs, by their nature, will potentially be of interest to a wide range of partners; the process of developing a stakeholder map as set out in Figure 3.1 (page 45) will help to prioritize the importance of the various potential partners. It is also difficult to define what is meant by the term 'partner' or 'member'. First, however, some general comments.

If it is envisaged that the PPP will be a fairly loose structure whose primary task is likely to be holding strategic discussions and developing policies rather than carrying out executive action, then membership can be reasonably wide; inclusivity is an essential characteristic of a successful PPP (particularly where policy development is concerned) and adoption of a wide membership satisfies this criteria. However there are two principal dangers to this approach:

- the PPP rapidly becomes too large and unwieldy;
- it becomes difficult to maintain an appropriate balance of power.

For example many initiatives in the economic or housing arenas require the active support of the private sector; that sector must therefore be strongly represented on any relevant PPP board. Equally however there is a wide range of voluntary or community groups who will wish to participate; if all of these are included and they can collectively outweigh the private sector then the latter will rapidly lose interest. Similarly, on an educational PPP it is important that the educational professionals do not outweigh the other sectors. Local Strategic Partnerships (LSPs) are particularly prone to suffer from this imbalance – there is an inclination to invite representation from the widest possible range of bodies, some of whom may have a relatively small, but vocal, constituency. In effect the activists start to outweigh the silent majority.

Achieving the correct balance of membership is difficult. Perhaps the most pragmatic approach is to recognize from the outset that there are two categories of potential members:

- the core or key members (partners) who will be required to make the major resource contribution to (and benefit most from) the work of the PPP; and
- the associate members (partners) whose views and inputs will be valuable but whose contribution to, and benefit from, the PPP will be less. They might, however, include some key community leaders in their management structure whom the PPP will wish to keep on side. The identification of possible associate members is as much about reducing potential opposition as about generating positive support.

In addition, regardless of the formal membership structure, there will be other organizations with a peripheral interest in the work of a PPP; their desire is to be kept informed rather than to have any formal participation. In effect they form the wider stakeholder group and are not really partners as such.

If this is acknowledged from the outset it makes it much easier to develop structural proposals. The core members would be the founder members of any company or partnership structure, and would always be represented on any boards set up to run the PPP. The associate members (the number of which could be much more flexible) could have consultative rights and perhaps limited representation on boards; the wider stakeholder group can be kept informed and consulted from time to time. All of this can be written into the relevant documentation (partnership deeds, contractual arrangements, company articles etc) at the outset. Figure 5.1 shows this approach diagrammatically.

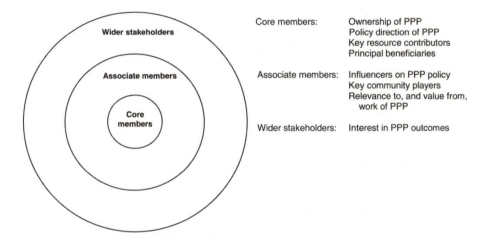

Figure 5.1 Membership of a PPP

The above comments are general in nature but can be applied slightly differently to each category of PPP.

1. Statutory based partnerships
In some cases the relevant legislation will specify the membership of a statutory based partnership; in other cases there will be greater freedom. For example the Crime and Disorder Act requires the 'responsible authorities' to work with 'other local agencies'; the responsible authorities are defined as the local police area, the police authority, the local authority, the fire authority and primary care trusts. These therefore are the 'core' members responsible for running the partnership. Other local agencies are not defined but most partnerships involve for example the probation service and the chamber of commerce ('associate' members). The 2002 Survey of Local Strategic Partnerships (published 2003) reported that 78 per cent of the respondents distinguished between core and non-core (associate) members, but the interpretation of the terms 'core' and 'members' varied considerably so the resultant data is difficult to interpret

(Table 7 of the Survey). The Survey listed 37 different categories of members; there were 20 categories listed as public organizations – these ranged from local authorities (members of 100 per cent of partnerships) to the Armed Forces (represented on 1 per cent). In the private sector categories, chambers of commerce or equivalent were members of virtually all LSPs, while an umbrella voluntary group was also a member of over 90 per cent of partnerships (Table 8). In terms of individual representation local authorities had the maximum number, as might be expected – the average number of local authority representatives on a LSP being 4 (Table 9). Because of the differences in defining the term 'member' it is difficult to give an average size of an LSP in core or associate membership terms but it is clear that many of them are very large bodies and relatively few are smaller than 20. This inevitably makes the management of LSPs difficult and 74 per cent indicated that they had an executive board of some sort (Table 11).

2.   Voluntary based partnerships

It is much more difficult to access data about the size and nature of the membership of voluntary based partnerships because of their range and variety. There is however some data on economic partnerships because most of them have developed a formal role in response to the creation of regional economic strategies (indeed in the East Midlands they are required to seek accreditation from the RDA). Some specific examples are given in the accompanying panel but it is noticeable that there is no consistency in private sector representation: in some partnerships representative bodies such as chambers of commerce are the private sector member; in others individual companies are members; while in others there is a combination of the two. As with Local Strategic Partnerships the number of members appears to range considerably although the higher membership numbers (those with 30 plus) probably include what has been categorized above as associate. This pattern is repeated in other partnerships – for example the South East Climate Change Partnership has about 40 members, the majority of whom are from public sector organizations but with some individual private sector companies and representative organizations.

3.   Commercially based partnerships

Membership of commercially based PPPs is generally much easier to determine. While the core members will be the partners contracted to deliver a particular project or service (the prime contractor and the relevant public body) there could be subcontractors involved in substantial parts of the work and they may therefore be associate members. There may also be more than one department of the public agency concerned. In some cases, such as the delivery of housing and support services to the elderly, representation from the consumer group might be appropriate (although they may only be in attendance and prohibited from participating in executive decision making).

CASE STUDIES: Classification of stakeholders

The accompanying text gives details of the results of the 2002 statistical survey of LSP membership; it can be seen that most LSPs have adopted a comprehensive approach to membership and manage their activities with the help of a small executive committee of some sort. The majority of voluntary based partnerships have adopted the same approach. The *Bedfordshire and Luton Economic Development Partnership* holds a large standing conference on a quarterly basis to which all stakeholders are invited and which provides overall strategic guidance to the executive. In the *Portsmouth and South East Hants Partnership* the associate members meet about three times a year for the same purpose. The *Northamptonshire Partnership* has four core partners (the County Council, the Learning and Skills Council, University College Northampton and the Chamber of Commerce) who are the members of the company but a much wider group of *associate* partners meet regularly. The *South East Climate Change Partnership* holds an annual forum open to any interested organization – that forum acts as an AGM and elects an executive committee which manages the partnership's work over the following year. The various studies on service delivery partnerships emphasize the value of involving elected members on the partnership board partly for accountability reasons but also to ensure that the consumers' view is properly represented, and to provide strong political support.

The question of membership therefore needs to be approached in a pragmatic way – what is appropriate for a particular PPP proposal? What is meant by the term 'membership'? Could the concept of 'core' and 'associate' membership work? Is it useful to develop the idea of a wider 'stakeholder group' to which the partnership could report occasionally? These issues need to be fully explored and clarified by the steering group before they are considered more widely. These discussions will need to take account of the expectations of the potential partners; some organizations may only be willing to participate if they are full (or core) members. However it will be important to emphasize to them during the initial discussions that core membership carries a responsibility, either in a financial or promotional sense. The effectiveness of a PPP will depend to a considerable extent on the commitment of the core members which must be demonstrated in some way. Equally the potential associate members or wider stakeholders will need to be reassured that they are not being treated as second class but are being treated realistically. This whole process of negotiation with potential partners is often a very delicate one requiring considerable interpersonal skills from the chair and champion. In the final analysis the PPP must work effectively and not be hamstrung by a 'membership' concept which makes this impossible. Having said that however the initial definition of membership will need to be sufficiently flexible to enable subsequent change as the partnership develops; in some cases it may well be appropriate to amend the core membership to reflect changing circumstances. It is therefore essential that the basic 'terms' of core membership (their responsibilities) are clear from the outset.

ROLE AND APPOINTMENT OF THE CHAIR

One of the most challenging aspects in developing structural proposals for a PPP is that of determining the role of the chair and how to fill the post. There is always the danger that either the chair of the initial steering group (or the PPP champion) will just drift into the role without proper consideration.

It is important that this should not happen – the skills required in the partnership development process are different from those required in the operational phase. In the development phase the chair of the steering group is concerned with marketing the concept and brokering initial structural or organizational issues. In the operational phase the emphasis changes; while the chair continues to act as the public face of the PPP, the marketing and brokering elements become less important and are replaced by the need to oversee the management of the PPP (including chairing the board, the composition of which is likely to be somewhat different from the group of enthusiasts making up the initial steering group). The precise nature and responsibilities of the chair will be different for each PPP (indeed in some cases the role and choice of chair will be predetermined by legislation or contractual arrangements) but there are a number of key elements common to all PPPs:

- The chair will be the 'face of the partnership' and therefore needs to be an individual with the right personal standing and credibility to ensure that the PPP is perceived as being independent from any particular partner.

- The chair must be able to command the respect of all the partners (both in an individual and organizational sense) and needs to be familiar with the management structures and organisational constraints of the individual partners.

- The chair must be able to chair a board which is likely to have a wide range of personalities and levels of ability – nominations to the board will come from a number of different organizations and board members will not necessarily be chosen by ability per se but as partner representatives.

- The chair will be the line manager of whatever executive structure is established; this will vary depending on the nature of the PPP but it is important that there is clarity in the reporting line and that the chair has the necessary management skills.

In those cases where the nature of the role and the choice of chair is open to discussion the steering group will need to develop outline proposals for negotiation with the potential partners; ultimately it will be for the core partners, once identified, to own the role and have confidence in the way it is carried out. A key point to be considered at the outset is whether the chair should always come from one sector (or partner), or whether the role should rotate amongst the sectors. (It is assumed that once in post the individual should act in an independent way when operating on behalf of the partnership.) There are pros and cons to both approaches; a rotational system sends a clear 'partnership' message but does have the potential for discontinuity in the partnership's business and relations with key stakeholders (which can be off-set by a strong executive director). On the other hand keeping the role in one sector also sends a message – it could be reserved for a sector perceived as independent (for example a partnership dealing with health or community matters could always be chaired by someone from the private sector rather than from either the health or local authority sectors). Partnerships have differed in their approach to this option – for example 81 per cent of the Local Strategic Partnerships in the 2002 Survey reported that the chair came from the local authority (Table 10 of the Survey) although this may change as LSPs mature, while most of the economic partnerships appear to have a chair from the private sector (and, in some cases such as the Hampshire Economic Partnership, are required to do so by their articles).

In parallel with developing ideas on the nature and role of the post where there is freedom of action, the steering group will need to consider any terms and conditions to be adopted since these can cause subsequent difficulties. Two particular issues need clarification at the outset – the term of office and method of appointment. As far as the term of office is concerned the most practical approach is to adopt a specific term relevant to the work of the PPP in question (one year, two years or even five years). This works well if the appointed chair is either independent or has an unlimited term of office from their nominating body but can cause problems if the chair's nomination to the board is dependent upon outside factors (such as elections to a local authority or to a nominating body). It is important not to make assumptions which can subsequently be misinterpreted but to develop clear proposals (if only in principle) for agreement by the initial members.

The second area requiring prior thought is the issue of how to appoint a chair. This will depend to some extent on whether it is envisaged that the post will always be filled from one sector or will rotate. There are a number of different ways of doing so but the most important principles are openness and clarity in order to ensure the confidence of all partners. The following different approaches have been tried and seem to have worked (in the sense of being acceptable to partners):

1. In some cases it may be appropriate to advertise publicly. Provided all the core members of the PPP are represented in the selection process (or if not,

have agreed to be bound by it) this can prove to be very successful. It demonstrates the independence of the post and also has the advantage of not disturbing the balance of the board.

2. If a representative from any sector is eligible then a periodic election by board members from amongst themselves is appropriate.

3. A nomination procedure whereby one sector nominates the chair from amongst their representatives for a specific period.

4. Where rotation is agreed a rotational nomination from each sector.

Public advertisement (1) has a cost to it and has to be handled with sensitivity – some individuals whom the core members might wish to attract will not respond willingly to a public advertisement and will need to be approached diplomatically, probably by the chair of the steering group. The object of the exercise is to generate the strongest possible field; once assembled the candidates will need to be assessed impartially against the agreed criteria for the post.

CASE STUDIES: The role and appointment of a PPP's chair

As might be expected, service delivery partnerships are generally chaired by the relevant public authority – for example the Leader of the *Milton Keynes Council* chairs the strategy board set up to oversee the work of the service delivery partnership. As noted in the accompanying text, most Local Strategic Partnerships currently have local authority nominees as their chair but this position may change – the 2002 Survey reported that 15 per cent of LSPs had either agreed the rotation principle or were considering doing so. *Hastings Local Strategic Partnership* is one which has already agreed to this principle with sectoral nominees serving for a one-year term. As a general rule it appears that economic partnerships specify that the chair must be from the private sector – for example this is the position in the *Northamptonshire Partnership*, the *Kent and Medway Economic Board*, and the *Hampshire Economic Partnership*. The *Milton Keynes Economic Partnership* on the other hand rotates the chair between the public and private sectors for a two-year term. Terms of office vary with some partnerships having no fixed term (such as in *Northamptonshire* or *Buckinghamshire*) but three years is specified by *Bedfordshire and Luton* and *Hampshire*.

The other options are cost-free but can suffer from the charge of exclusivity, particularly from the wider stakeholder group (less so in the case of (4)). If these options are adopted then board members will need to agree beforehand on a couple of points – first, will the chair when appointed retain a 'sectoral' vote or is the chair to be denied a vote and required to act impartially? This could have a significant effect on the work of the board if it adopts a procedure based on formal voting. Secondly, will unanimity from all the partners be required before a nominee from one partner is appointed chair? These issues may seem trivial but it is important that they are addressed at the outset in view of the potentially fragile nature of a PPP at the start of its life. It is also helpful if the requirements of the post, the term of office and appointment process can be written into an appropriate document at the outset (such as board minutes, partnership deed, company articles or contractual arrangements) since this will avoid conflict in the future – goodwill may be in plentiful supply at the establishment of the PPP but may have dissipated somewhat by the time subsequent chairs are appointed.

THE POWERS AND FUNCTIONS OF THE BOARD

One of the more challenging aspects of a PPP's formation is likely to be that of defining the powers and functions of the board; in this context the term 'board' means the group that will have the ultimate responsibility for the work of the PPP. In some cases this will be a 'partnership board' while in others this will be a formal 'board of directors' operating under the Companies Act. Normally the board will be made up of the representatives of the core members, sometimes supplemented by representatives from the associate members.

Traditionally there has been a fairly clear differentiation between the way that public sector bodies have been managed and the way that private sector organizations have been; this stemmed from their respective ownership. Organizations in the public sector were owned by the community and operated on the community's behalf by elected individuals; their aim was to provide services to the public and not to generate profits. In the private sector, companies were owned by shareholders and operated on their behalf by directors whom they appointed; their aim was to provide a profit (or dividend) for the shareholders through the sale of goods or services.

This basic ownership distinction remains but, as noted in the first chapter, the operational distinctions between the two sectors have become much more blurred as the financial context under which a modern economy functions has changed. Some public institutions, with no personal shareholders, effectively trade as if they are private bodies (ranging from public corporations owned by the government, such as the Post Office, to health trusts), while some privately owned organizations (such as universities and many voluntary bodies) depend to a large extent on public funds. PPPs are a new type of organization which effectively sit in the middle between the two traditional extremes.

The changing nature of today's organizations has however resulted in the development of a range of different governance arrangements and operational emphasis although the same differences in approach remain. The organizations in what can still be called the traditional public sector continue to rely on elected individuals for leadership; inevitably such bodies tend to operate on a relatively short time frame concentrating on the efficient delivery of services, the aim being to deliver a manifesto to ensure subsequent re-election; long-term strategy tends to assume a lower importance. Purely private sector organizations, on the other hand, tend to adopt a governance structure which emphasizes that the role of the board is long-term strategy with considerable day-to-day freedom for the executive. Organizations in the growing middle category, such as PPPs, find themselves adopting a variety of approaches. Some see their board as being very strategic in nature while others are much more operational; to some extent this will depend on whether the PPP is primarily a policy development vehicle or one which delivers services, but this is not universally true. For example the nature of the membership of the boards of Local Strategic Partnerships, which are basically policy development partnerships, often means that long-term strategic issues are discussed in minute detail rather than being considered within a broad picture.

CASE STUDIES: The nature and powers of a partnership board

The increasing use of a formal company structure by voluntary based partnerships has meant that such partnerships have had to become more specific in the nature and role of their board. The *Buckinghamshire Economic Partnership*'s articles require the board to have a majority from the private sector, while the *Hampshire Economic Partnership*'s board is required to represent various interests specified in the articles. The legal powers assigned to such boards appear to have been very broadly defined and based on the various model articles which are published by a number of organizations, the only variation being in the company's objectives. Service delivery partnerships are, in general, not incorporated as a separate entity (although major new delivery organizations such as for the *National Air Traffic System* do have their own legal structure). In *Norfolk* a partnership board has been set up to oversee the delivery of various IT and financial services by a private contractor; the board is 'the custodian of the relationship developed by the contract; monitors progress and performance; decides on changes in the scope of services to be provided; and agrees a three-year strategy and one-year business plan'. It has senior membership from both parties and meets quarterly. A very similar board exists in *Milton Keynes*. Both boards appear to have been given considerable freedom by their parent authority and are supported by various operational arrangements.

Both traditional extremes are now changing fairly rapidly. In the public sector the government is emphasizing the importance of strategic development (hence the establishment of LSPs) and is requiring public organizations to demonstrate clearer executive responsibility (hence the development of cabinet government in local councils); the creation of executive agencies in central government is another example of this trend. In the private sector the role of the Board of Directors has come under considerable scrutiny in the last few years, with boards being asked to assume much more accountability for a company's day-to-day activities.

This changing contextual background is having an impact on the ways PPPs are governed. The idea of establishing a purely nominal board with little direct control over the activities of a PPP executive is no longer acceptable – boards must be more closely involved in the work of the partnership and must demonstrate a greater degree of accountability. Figure 5.2 illustrates the spectrum of options which are worth considering when developing a PPP.

The passive board	The certifying board	The engaged board	The operating board
• traditional 'company' model • limited activity • concentrates on strategy • ratifies management's action • meets quarterly or less	• questions management's proposals • gives prior approval to proposals • actively reports back to partners • likely to meet monthly	• operates alongside management in developing proposals • uses own contacts to supplement management	• develops own ideas • instructs management on regular basis • exercises direct control over finances • meets frequently

Figure 5.2   Options for a PPP Board

Clearly there are overlaps between each type of board, and it is also possible that the nature of a PPP board might change as it develops – it is likely to move from the right to the left hand side of the spectrum as the board develops confidence in the executive. However in developing proposals to put to potential partners the steering group will need to have a fairly clear idea of which model is envisaged in the longer term (or steady state). The nature and composition of a partnership board not only affects the way a partnership is managed but also sends out a signal to the wider community on how the partnership sees itself. It is therefore important that the steering group considers these issues at an early stage; the approach which is adopted will also of course have an impact on the consequential decisions to be taken on the supporting infrastructure of the partnership.

In order to help define the nature of the board which is proposed it is helpful to bear in mind the range of functions with which the board is likely to become involved and to consider how much involvement in each is envisaged:

1. setting the overall vision and strategy;

2. developing a detailed business plan, including targets;

3. ensuring appropriate resources;

4. appointing and managing executive staff (or ensuring appropriate contractual arrangements);

5. receiving, approving and auditing financial reports, budgets and so on;

6. ensuring compliance with legal and partnership requirements;

7. developing and monitoring accountability arrangements;

8. promoting the work of the PPP.

Some PPP boards will wish to become closely involved in all aspects of these functions; others will tend to concentrate on fewer. For example a LSP will concentrate on 1 and 8 and may be less interested in other functions; an economic partnership with an executive role is likely to be more interested in 2 to 6; a commercially based partnership will be more concerned with 2, 3 and 5.

The development of initial proposals in respect of the role of the board helps two other aspects of the partnership development strategy – the choice of an appropriate executive and management structure (see below), and the choice of individual nominees to serve on the board by the partners. Partners will inevitably tend to nominate their board representative in accordance with their own internal procedures – for example a chamber of commerce may have already identified an individual to represent it on local partnerships, while a local authority may always insist on its representative being from the ruling party (or may insist on a political balance in its nominations).

It follows that the chair and champion, in their discussions with potential partners, may not be in a position to insist on any criteria for board nominees; however if there is a chance to influence a choice then it is worth emphasising the following:

- Collectively the board must enjoy the confidence of all the partners; individual board members must therefore understand and support the objectives of the PPP.

- Individually the board members should be able to commit their organizations to any agreements made at the board.

- Individual board members should undertake the primary responsibility for reporting back to their organization and ensuring accountability to partners.

- Board members will need to recognize and accept that the modus operandi of the PPP may well be somewhat different from that adopted in their own organization; procedures which are appropriate to a council or public company are not necessarily suitable for use in a multi sector partnership.

- It is useful if board members can bring a specific individual skill or relevant personal network to the work of the board.

The effectiveness of a partnership's board will depend on a number of factors but the quality of the chair and the members will play a vital role. It is therefore worth trying to influence the nomination process if at all possible. It is interesting to note that, in their review of strategic partnerships published in 2001, the New Local Government Network stated that their survey showed that 'a partnership board ... was considered desirable ... with executive members as a mechanism for providing corporate leadership' (Page 7).

INFRASTRUCTURE TO SUPPORT THE PPP

All PPPs, of whatever category, will need to develop their own infrastructure to support their work. At one end of the spectrum the PPP will employ staff (at both senior and junior level), occupy its own offices and project a very physical presence in the community; at the other end the PPP will subcontract all its supporting arrangements to one of the partners. There can be a variety of arrangements between these two extremes.

The choice of infrastructure arrangements will reflect the nature of the PPP and proposals will need to be developed by the steering group alongside their suggestions on the PPP's structure and role of the board. Their recommendation on infrastructure is more than one just based on operational convenience – the approach which a PPP adopts will send out a strong signal to both the partners and wider stakeholders. If it is decided that a PPP needs a very visible place in the community, and needs to have the capacity to undertake strategy development or direct action in-house, then the PPP is likely to need to appoint a senior executive to lead the organization (an executive director). This can be the case right across the range of PPPs – a statutory based Local Strategic Partnership may wish to take the lead in developing a community strategy rather than relying on integrating proposals from partners or specialist strategic partnerships. A voluntary based PPP such as a learning partnership may wish to develop and manage its own initiatives, while a commercially based partnership may want to appoint a senior executive to undertake a rigorous scrutiny of a contractor's performance. The strong leadership approach carries obvious risks. Apart from the cost implications the role of executive director will need to have sufficient authority to attract good candidates. However it must be remembered that the authority of a partnership can only be derived by agreement from the partners (unless there is a contractual commitment on the partnership – for example if the partnership has been established to receive funds from a third party to deliver specific services). Thus, if choosing to appoint a strong executive director, it is essential to clarify the nature of the relationship with the partners and recruit accordingly; it is important that the individual recognizes the parameters of the role.

The alternative to the adoption of a strong leadership approach is to operate at a minimum administrative support level and rely on support from one of the partners. This approach has the obvious weakness of a lack of independence and the danger of relying on one of the partners to deliver.

There is an inevitable tendency, particularly at the outset, for PPPs to adopt the minimalist approach for two reasons. First, partners will be reluctant to agree to anything which might be perceived as reducing or challenging their own roles; and secondly, there is a cost factor. Even if the partnership itself does not act as the employer (with all the consequential long-term employment implications) the direct salary costs of a senior executive will have to be met by the partners (together possibly with appropriate support staff).

Assuming that it is decided to appoint an executive director of some sort, the steering group will need to develop for discussion with potential partners a reasonably detailed job description as part of the partnership development strategy. Strong interpersonal skills and political awareness will need to feature highly on the required personal characteristics, alongside the relevant professional and managerial skills. Once the nature of the post has been decided then a choice has to be made on how to fill it; the options are to seek applicants through open advertisement or to restrict the field to the wider stakeholder group of interested organizations. In practice open advertisement appears to be the approach most frequently adopted – this demonstrates a partnership's desire for independence and makes a very public statement to the wider stakeholder group. In practical terms the open advertisement route does not rule out applications from the stakeholder organizations and has the advantage of widening the field.

In the same way that the role of permanent chair is different from that of the chair of the steering group, it is important that the new role of executive director is differentiated from that of partnership champion or project manager. The latter role is very much about developing structures and delivering the partnership development strategy. The new role is essentially a management role and the executive director will have a major management task; this might include policy development (if that is the

CASE STUDIES: The executive leadership and staffing of partnerships

Statutory partnerships are generally supported by the officers in the relevant public authorities. Crime and community safety partnerships are almost always supported by a joint police/local authority team with the police rotating appropriate officers into the role. The 2002 Survey of Local Strategic Partnerships reported that 28 per cent of partnerships had their own dedicated support staff but many of these were funded through the neighbourhood renewal programme covered under the auspices of the LSP. The survey also indicated that the median number of dedicated support staff was 1.2, including those managing NRF programmes (Tables 16 and 17 in the Survey). Voluntary partnerships such as economic partnerships are developing rather more robust structures. Most of those surveyed had an executive director type post with a small but growing staff. For example the *Northamptonshire Partnership* has a Chief Executive supported by an Operations Manager and four Development Managers. In the *Thames Valley Economic Partnership*, which puts a major emphasis on inward investment, there is a team of four dedicated to this function reporting to the Chief Executive who also has a small team working on more general strategic issues. The emphasis in service delivery partnerships is obviously somewhat different; the contractor will have their own team dedicated to deliver the required services but it is also essential that the client develops their own 'matching' team. The Deputy Chief Executive of the *London Borough of Islington* was quoted in the NLGN's review of strategic partnerships as saying 'Having an Assistant Director with client responsibility matters makes a real difference to the development of partnerships, problem resolution and facilitation.'

primary role of the PPP), and could include line management of executive action (either directly or through contract management). It will certainly require budgetary and committee management skills, and the executive director will also need to take the lead in communicating with the wider stakeholder group and community. This latter function, which is vitally important if the PPP is to be successful, will have to be carried out by the chair if it is decided not to proceed with the executive director style of infrastructure. However, while this emphasis on the management aspects of the role is to be expected it should not be at the expense of the negotiating and influencing aspects which are at the heart of the PPP champion's role; those aspects will continue to be important.

In view of the somewhat delicate issues involved in determining an appropriate infrastructure for a PPP it is sometimes sensible to make a short-term or interim appointment in the first instance (say for a 12-month period) in order to help develop the parameters of the role. While it is tempting to ask the partnership champion to continue to serve in this capacity, this can be counter-productive in that the tasks to be performed in actually setting up the partnership are somewhat different from those required in developing the strategy. A secondment from a partner is sometimes the best interim solution providing the secondee is reasonably independently minded.

RESOURCING A PARTNERSHIP

It is important to distinguish the basic resourcing of a partnership (the day-to-day running costs) from the funding of a partnership's programme. Basic resource costs include salaries and office costs; they also include meeting costs and the costs of any routine expenditure authorised by the PPP board such as the production and management of a website or PR activities. While a detailed budget and business plan will probably not be appropriate at this stage in a partnership's development, the steering group will need to make a realistic assessment of the costs involved so that the potential core partners understand the likely scale of their commitment.

The question of how the basic resource costs of a PPP should be met will depend on the circumstances of each PPP. A statutory based partnership, such as a Crime and Community Safety Partnership, will probably be serviced by officers from the police and local authority; the costs are therefore likely to be met by those two bodies and the other parties involved (such as the chamber of commerce) will not be asked to contribute. The situation is different with voluntary based partnerships – many appear to have adopted a subscription type approach, with the core partners contributing an agreed share of the costs (not necessarily on an equal basis). Commercially based partnerships are likely to be supported through the agreed contractual arrangements (for PFI or service delivery partnerships), or by the initial sponsoring organization (such as a housing association). It is important that there should be some continuity in respect of the basic resourcing of a partnership – a PPP, like any organization, will need to plan over a reasonable time scale (say three years). It follows that the chair and champion, in their discussions with potential partners, should endeavour to obtain promises (at least in principle) of medium-term financial support.

In addition to basic resources a PPP may need access to programme funding (on either a long-term or per-project basis). This can be provided either as part of the original partnership agreement or, more usually, through ad hoc grants from partners or third parties. This simplistic statement hides the fact that there are often significant costs involved in generating such funds – considerable time and effort often has to be devoted to writing proposals for such funds (from say the European Union) and it is helpful to clarify at the outset of a PPP's existence how, in principle, it is envisaged that these costs will be met if and when they arise.

SUMMARY

- The steering group will need to define what is meant by the term 'membership'.

- It is often helpful to categorize membership under three headings – core members (who will own the PPP, direct the policy, be the key resource contributors and beneficiaries), associate members (whose influence on both the work of the PPP and the community will be important) and the wider stakeholder group.

- It is useful to build the operational structure of the PPP around these three categories and it is important that the potential members understand and accept these distinctions.

- It is important to recognize that the initial membership structure may change over time; clear definitions of the role and responsibility of each category of member need to be set out from the outset.

- The chair of the PPP is a crucial appointment and it is important to develop the principles underpinning the role and how it will be filled at the outset. The chair of the steering group should not become the permanent chair without an assessment against the new requirements.

- The nature of the board needs to be clear from the start. Often the board will move from being very operational and hands-on in the initial stages of a PPP's life to being more of a certifying board as confidence is built up in the PPP's operations.

- An early decision needs to be made on the nature of the infrastructure – is it intended that the PPP will develop a fairly independent life of its own or will it rely on the staff of the partners?

- There needs to be clarity over the role of executive director and the relationship between that role and the partners. As with the post of chair the partnership champion should not automatically become the executive director but should be assessed against the requirements of the post and other candidates.

- There needs to be clarity of how the basic resourcing costs of the PPP will be met over an adequate timescale.

CHAPTER 6

Managing a Partnership's Business

Regardless of their nature and why they were established, PPPs are fragile creatures – their long-term success will depend upon the creation of mutual confidence between the partnership and the individual partners. Partnerships are the creatures of the partners and it is therefore essential that they should never be seen to challenge the role of the partners but should be seen as adding value. Furthermore, it takes time to gain that confidence – even if the negotiations to establish a PPP have gone very well it cannot be assumed that the partnership will enjoy the full confidence of the partners from day one.

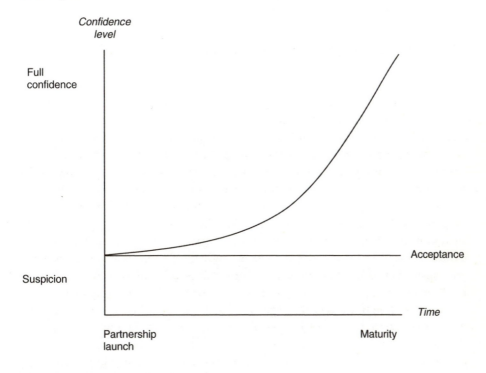

Figure 6.1 Confidence level in a PPP

Figure 6.1 illustrates the point – hopefully the graph will show a steady improvement as the PPP matures; indeed, the rate of improvement should increase as time passes and confidence grows. However do not be surprised if the graph sometimes dips below the 'acceptance' line, particularly in the early stages; it is only natural for the partners to be suspicious of the new organization. It is much more concerning if the graph dips below the line after the partnership has been operating for some time.

It is therefore important that that those responsible for managing the partnership, particularly the chair and executive director (or equivalent), take care over deciding how the partnership is to be managed once it has been established. It cannot be assumed that what works with one particular partner will be acceptable practice to the others. Each PPP will have its own unique characteristics and will need to work out the most effective and acceptable modus operandi to meet its needs; this chapter sets out some guidelines which should help the process.

UNDERLYING PRINCIPLES

There are two key principles which should underlie the operational arrangements of a PPP, namely, *clarity* and *balance.*

There needs to be absolute *clarity* between what a partnership is going to do, how it is going to do it and what is to be undertaken by the individual partners. While the basic distinctions should be fairly clear from the objectives of the PPP, the detailed arrangements may well not have been thought through in the initial discussions. For example there will be no problems in deciding that a local strategic partnership will be responsible for developing a community strategy; almost certainly however there will be differences of opinion over the precise relationship between the LSP and the preparation of the supporting strategies. While there may be general agreement that such strategies should be the responsibility of specialist partnerships or groups (such as health or learning partnerships), there may well be differences of opinion over the relationship between the various partnerships. Will the contributory strategies have to be signed off by the LSP? Or will they be accepted without further discussion? If every recommendation from a specialist partnership becomes subject to the whims of a more broadly based LSP then the specialist contributors will rapidly lose interest, to the detriment of all. Clarifying the detailed terms of the relationship between the LSP and the other partnerships therefore becomes crucially important. Equally a PPP set-up to deliver a service must be clear about the limits of the services envisaged – it must not start straying into services delivered by one of the partners. It is useful therefore to develop a protocol of some sort setting out the boundaries of activity between a PPP and partner organisations. *Clarity* also needs to underpin the roles of a PPP's board members and officers – when acting on behalf of the PPP they must divorce themselves from their 'constituency' role. This is often very difficult, particularly in the early stages where there will be lingering doubts about the PPP's role.

The question of *balance* is equally important. As indicated above confidence in a PPP can only be developed if the individual partners do not feel threatened in any way. A partnership's strength is the additionality which it provides. There must therefore be a balance between what a partnership does and what the individual partners do. It is important to resist the temptation to ask a partnership to undertake an ever-widening range of activities (particularly if they are complex or politically difficult) which gradually eat into the role of one of the partners. It is also important that the creation of a partnership should not become an excuse for 'passing the buck'. Partners must maintain their own integrity and continue to take decisions on matters which are intrinsic to their own existence. Stakeholder confidence in both the partnership and the individual partners can only be maintained if there is an acceptable accountability balance.

These principles do not mean that every issue which comes up is an 'either/or' one. There will be many instances where it is perfectly legitimate for both a partnership and an individual partner to have a view. Hopefully those views will coincide, but this will not always be the case. For example local economic conditions may lead all the relevant organizations to support an improved transport infrastructure; the local authority may favour a solution emphasizing improvements in public transport while the business community may prefer additional road building. In practice the solution is likely to combine both policies. The partnership approach is to emphasize the common ground – the need for improved infrastructure – and to work towards a solution which incorporates elements of both public transport and increased road capacity. The council and the business community can then argue for their own preferences when individual projects come to be considered by the funding agencies.

BUSINESS MANAGEMENT PROCESS

One of the most influential aspects of any organization's management process is that of managing the agenda (in both the broad sense and the more restricted sense of the agenda for specific meetings) and setting the priorities for the organization. In the private sector this is a fairly straightforward process – the chief executive, working with the chair and the executive team, sets the agenda for discussion and approval by the board; the executive team then gets on with the delivery process. In the public sector the situation is not so clear cut. In central and local government the theory is that overall strategy and prioritization is led by the elected representatives (often supplemented by specialist advisors), while operational matters are the responsibilities of the appropriate chief officer. In practice there is considerable overlap which, in the case of local authorities, has been complicated further with the advent of the cabinet system under which a small group of elected members have assumed much greater control over authorities' day-to-day activities. The position in health, education, and voluntary sector bodies varies but tends towards the latter model with considerable authority vested in elected representatives albeit often operating with close guidance from their officers.

This difference in approach makes the task of agenda setting more difficult in a PPP because of the nature of partnership. The private sector will expect the partnership's executive director to take the lead (perhaps in consultation with the chair), while most of the other representatives around the table will anticipate that they will have an important role to play. There can be no hard and fast rules applying to all PPPs – like most things with PPPs the solution will depend on the particular circumstances of each PPP and the personality and strengths of the individuals involved. In general however it is true to say that board members will expect to have a say both in developing policy and in setting priorities within that policy regardless of whether or not the board decides to become very hands on in operational matters (see Figure 5.2). Board members of all PPPs will wish to play a prominent role in strategy development and in setting objectives to deliver that strategy; they will want to feel that they have been properly consulted and have made a contribution rather than just been used as a rubber stamping body. This means that extra care will need to be taken in the preparation of papers for the board – they will need to be fairly discursive and offer options for consideration rather than to make bald recommendations after a brief summary of the facts. Skill in drafting board papers in this way should therefore be an important part of the job description of the executive director – influencing skills need to be both oral and written. Since the chair is the individual who is likely to have the closest contact with the governing structures of the individual partners it follows that it is essential that the chair and executive director develop a close relationship from the start, and work together to convince the other board members of the most acceptable way forward. They need to be at one in terms of the strategic objectives and way forward for the partnership. Any differences in approach between the two will inevitably lead to a loss of partnership coherence and leadership. This once again illustrates the need to ensure that the selection process for both posts must ensure personal compatability between the two individuals – good interpersonal skills need to be high on the selection criteria for both posts.

The previous chapter emphasized the need to ensure clarity over the role of the support structure for a PPP. Many will choose to go down the route of a fairly robust structure headed by a reasonably influential executive director of some sort; others may choose to rely on a more low key structure. Regardless of the structure adopted however there is one essential prerequisite if a PPP's agenda management is to be successful – the agenda must be drawn up in conjunction with the individual partners.

There should be no surprises on the partnership's agenda; neither the partners nor their individual representatives should be 'bounced' into discussing something about which they are unprepared. In effect the partnership must beware of taking on a life of its own – it must always remain a creature of its partners if it is to retain their confidence.

This implies that a PPP's leadership (the chair and executive director) must keep in constant contact with the individual partners. Circumstances will be different in each partnership but it is usually at officer level that this contact is maintained. For example the support structure for a Crime and Community Partnership is generally provided jointly by officers from the police and local authority; they will clarify issues of agenda management and ensure that their respective organizations know what matters are to be considered so that their representatives can respond positively at any partnership meetings. Where other organizations might have a role to play (such as the fire authority or business community) then it is essential that the secretariat advise them beforehand. The same is true of those partnerships involved in executive action such as the delivery of services – the relevant partnership officer will need to liaise with colleagues in partner organizations before proposing anything formally. In many areas of the country groups of officers from a range of local organizations meet regularly on either a formal or informal basis to discuss forward business and ensure complementarity of agenda management in their own organizations. This is a very useful and effective way of proceeding; indeed, it is often a good way of involving the full range of associate partners who may not normally attend board meetings. It also brings the executive director and other partnership staff into regular contact with partners. In this way the ethos of partnership working can be developed and spread throughout the community – the wider the range of the contributions to agenda management the better.

One of the inevitable consequences of this approach is to slow down the decision-making process in PPPs; it also means that an issue often has to be referred back to the individual partners before final partnership approval. This frequently creates irritation amongst members used to a more straightforward process but is a feature of partnership working. While this is generally a private sector complaint it is occasionally the public sector who becomes irritated – for example a chamber of commerce may feel that it has to consult its members on a specific policy issue (particularly over such thorny issues as parking or public transport) before the policy can be supported.

The policy of undertaking prior consultation over the agenda becomes slightly more difficult when the partnership is involved in developing strategy and has decided to adopt a strong support structure headed by a reasonably heavyweight executive director. Although (hopefully) the terms of reference given to an executive director on appointment will have made clear the need for constant consultation with partners, there will be an inevitable tendency for the executive director to submit detailed policy proposals direct to the partnership board without adequate pre-consultation with the individual partners (particularly if they have been used to this style of working previously). For example an executive director of an economic partnership might be tempted to respond directly to a government initiative on behalf of the partnership because of their own specialist knowledge or experience; such a response may be perfectly sensible but may not reflect the local 'political nuances' of the individual partners. Successful partnership working requires that an executive director, at whatever level, spends as much time as possible consulting (and hopefully convincing) the individual partners before bringing issues to the partnership board or responding on behalf of the partnership. In this connection it is often useful for a PPP executive director to be automatically invited to attend the relevant decision-making meetings in individual partners, if only in an advisory capacity. Both the PPP and the partners can then be pre-warned of forthcoming issues.

The example above again illustrates the need for a strong relationship between the chair and the executive director; the former can act as a sounding board for the latter and advise the director on the most appropriate pre-consultation process. It is the strength of this relationship, backed up by a coherent and consistent consultation process which will ensure the effective management of a partnership's agenda.

Prioritization within a partnership's agenda is an area where more board participation is to be encouraged. There is usually considerable scope for bargaining between the various sectors within a partnership once the main strategic objectives and outcomes have been agreed. Individual board members will wish to make a contribution and to influence the partnership's detailed activities. This is particularly true of public sector representatives who will wish to reflect the partnership's achievements, and their personal contribution thereto, in their subsequent election manifesto. Indeed the prioritization role is often the most important one in many partnerships – for example the overall agenda of a health partnership is set by central government but there is considerable local freedom on priorities. A service delivery partnership will have overall targets but there can be room for manoeuvre on which community groups should be given priority for the services in question.

A PPP's STRATEGIC PLAN

Like all organizations a PPP will need to produce two types of plan – a strategic plan covering the next 5–10 years and an annual business plan, although the nature of these needs to reflect the particular characteristics of partnership working. The strategic plan does not have to be produced annually but should probably be refreshed periodically and thoroughly re-written every few years. A PPP's first strategic plan will be based very much on the partnership development strategy (or delivery contract). The amount of detail which it will contain will vary from partnership to partnership – indeed it can be quite brief provided it is punchy – but it should include the following five elements:

- *The partnership's overall goal or objectives.* There should be a clear statement on what the partnership is setting out to achieve – what will be the outcome of its work over the next 5–10 years. This strategic objective needs to articulate the specific added value which the partnership is aiming to deliver. This can be a very aspirational statement which does not have to be expressed in specific numerical terms (although that is sometimes useful) but should be a clearly recognized goal supported by all the partners.

- *An outline of the partnership's work.* The strategic plan will need to indicate what activities the partnership proposes to undertake over the next few years to achieve the overall goal. The detail of each activity can be left to the annual business plan but the strategic plan should identify each and indicate why it is important – for example a learning partnership could identify the development of basic skills as a key component of its work because of the strategic need to achieve a balanced workforce, while the business plan would quantify this and set annual targets for each individual programme or partner.

- *An indication of the resource requirement.* Detailed costings and budgets will feature in the annual business plan but the strategic plan needs to give an idea of the resources that are likely to be required to deliver the range of activities envisaged and where these are expected to come from. Any anticipated changes in the balance of resources available to the partnership or its partners can be highlighted so that plans to adjust or reallocate resources can be discussed at an early stage.

- *Partnership evolution.* Since by definition a strategic plan covers a relatively long time period it is more than likely that the partnership will have to evolve to meet changing circumstances. It is important that a partnership indicates to the wider stakeholder group its willingness to evolve – a partnership structure must be dynamic if it is to continue to offer added value; new players will come on the scene; priorities will change and so on. A partnership must continue to be inclusive and its strategic plan should give some indication of how the original members see this happening.

- *Relationships with others.* In parallel with the need for a partnership to demonstrate a willingness to evolve is the need to make clear that the partnership will continue to develop and maintain close links with other organizations and to demonstrate accountability to the wider community.

A partnership needs to be seen to be working with others in a collaborative and non-threatening way and the strategic plan is a good vehicle to demonstrate this.

Every PPP's strategic plan will be different but the two principles to bear in mind when preparing one are: first, the need to demonstrate a partnership's clarity in its objectives and how it plans to achieve them; and secondly the need to show that it is a true partnership willing to work with others for the benefit of the community. Essentially the strategic plan is as much an opportunity to promote the value of partnership working as it is to provide a framework for the annual business planning process.

A PPP's ANNUAL BUSINESS PLAN

The annual business plan is the vehicle through which the strategic plan is delivered. It does not need to repeat the aspirations of the strategic plan but has to put the flesh on the strategy by setting out the detailed programme for each year and establishing clear targets against which the partnership and its employees can be measured; no organization can operate without such a plan. However as with the strategic plan the components of a PPP's business plan are slightly different from those which might be produced for either a public sector organization or a business. This is because of the importance of ensuring that the partnership elements are properly measured. The hard, or measurable, outputs can be categorized in a similar way to any other organization but the soft components will need to reflect the partnership and multi-sector nature of the PPP. Although each partnership will be different the principal topics which should be covered in a PPP's business plan are as follows:

- *Measurable outputs.* Every PPP needs specific deliverables. In the case of a partnership devoted primarily to strategy development the outputs would include both the publication (or annual updating) of the strategy itself and evidence of its acceptance by the partners and wider stakeholders. This latter point is particularly important; there is little purpose in producing a comprehensive strategy if it is subsequently ignored by the individual partners. There therefore needs to be a target which assesses the support of the partners for the strategy; for example, has the strategy been formally adopted by the partners? What evidence is there? (Is the strategy reflected in their own business plan?) Are the strategic targets reflected in the partners' own targets? Where the partnership is more concerned with executive action there will be specific service delivery targets; these could be at either partnership or individual partner level. The essential thing is to ensure consistency of outputs between the partnership and the partners; this reinforces the point that there must be regular contact between all those involved – a partnership is not there to impose targets on the partners but to ensure complementarity and, through complementarity, a better overall output.

- *Research/assessment reports.* All PPPs should undertake regular activities to underpin and validate their work. While all organizations should do this it is particularly important for a partnership because of the need to constantly re-emphasize the benefits of its additionality. Initial strategy development is likely to involve more academic research of some sort, but subsequent work will need to be done on the impact of the strategy; for example, have the targets in the local economic or health strategy resulted in specific local improvements? Have they been able to influence policy in a wider sense? Service delivery targets should be accompanied by an assessment of some sort to ensure that the services are actually delivering what was envisaged. It is also worth considering including under this heading work to assess the wider community's appreciation of a partnership's activities – one of the indications of a partnership's success is the acceptance of its value by the wider community or stakeholder group.

- *Finance.* Partnerships delivering executive functions will have a specific budget against which to report; strategy-oriented partnerships are likely to have somewhat looser financial objectives; indeed they may have fairly small budgets. However one particular issue which should feature in every PPP's business plan is the expected financial contribution from each partner to the basic running costs of the partnership. This is because it is important that a PPP, of whatever type, should enjoy the broadest possible range of support; it is equally important that a PPP should not rely on only one or two partners – not only is it then financially vulnerable but it also leads to the danger that the principal funders will suspect the other partners of not pulling their weight. Clarity over funding is very important in the partnership world.

- *Partner involvement.* It is useful to include targets setting out the expected degree of involvement by the partners in the business plan; at the end of the year the partnership board needs to be able to assess whether partners are playing their full part in the partnership and, if not, what remedial steps could be taken. This simple statement covers a very complex issue. At one level partner involvement can be measured in a straightforward way: number of meetings attended; reports generated to partner boards; specific action taken by the partners and so on. A more difficult (and, in many ways, more important) aspect to measure is the continuing 'emotional' support for the partnership. A PPP will often be launched with considerable commitment from the partners (perhaps based on the enthusiastic support from a particular individual) but maintaining this can be difficult. One possible way of measuring this is to ask the chair to present annually to the board a personal assessment of each partner's commitment to the PPP. While this approach has its dangers it does oblige the chair to continue to take a personal interest in the strength of the partnership; it also puts the partners 'on warning' that they need to be more than just a name at the table.

- *Working practices.* While similar to the previous component it is useful to try and set out some specific guidelines on working practices which should apply to the day-to-day activities of the PPP's own staff and their relationship with the staff of the individual partners. It is important that a close working relationship is maintained; setting specific targets in this area is difficult but again an annual assessment can be useful (perhaps from the chair or, if not, from the executive director).

- *Staff development.* Large organizations are accustomed to incorporating staff development objectives in their business plans. It is more difficult for a PPP but no less important. A PPP, by definition, is engaged in a cultural change process; it is developing new ways of working which inevitably puts a strain on the partnership staff. It follows that staff appointed to a PPP for the first time, or seconded by one of the partners, may need help in developing the different skills needed for successful partnership working. Secondments to other partnerships, to core partners, or to key stakeholders (such as regional bodies) can often be a very powerful development tool.

- *Accountability.* Every PPP must be able to continue to demonstrate its accountability to both the core partners and the wider stakeholder group. A PPP cannot exist without partners and there should be a regular review of how the partnership is maintaining its accountability; the next chapter discusses this in more detail.

Figure 6.2 summarizes these components in tabular form.

OPERATIONAL MANAGEMENT

Every PPP will develop its own style of operational management depending upon its circumstances. But there are a few general points to bear in mind when considering how to manage the day-to-day activities of a partnership. The tone of a PPP's management approach will be set by its board; Figure 5.2 (page 71) summarized the options which are available and the choice of option will then lead on to determining the style of support structure. However, whatever overall approach is adopted it is essential that true partnership working is inculcated into its activities.

CASE STUDIES: Developing strategic and annual business plans

The 2002 Survey of Local Strategic Partnerships showed that, at that time, most LSPs had not developed a formal planning structure – not unnaturally since they were still unsure about their long-term role and powers. Crime and Community Safety Partnerships have a longer track record and are more homogenous in nature given their specific responsibilities. As a result it has been possible for the Home Office to issue fairly comprehensive guidelines, and each partnership has to produce both strategic and annual business plans for submission to the relevant government regional office; they also have to produce an annual report in a prescribed form. Many of the voluntary partnerships are required to produce plans by their primary funding agency – for example EMDA requires the *Northamptonshire Partnership* to produce an annual plan geared to delivering the Regional Economic Strategy (RES). All the economic partnerships in the South East which receive core funding from SEEDA have to produce plans which incorporate the RES; most partnerships, however, publish a more comprehensive plan which identifies their more local priorities in addition to the RES priorities. The *Kent and Medway Economic Board* is a typical example – its annual business plan reflects its strategic economic framework which identifies the area's long-term goals and which is also updated annually.

	Nature of partnership	
Component	Strategy development	Executive delivery
Publication of strategy	X	
Approval of strategy by stakeholders	X	
Delivery of specific services		X
Research/assessment reports	X	X
Financial objectives	X	
Financial targets/budgets		X
Degree of partnership involvement by partners	X	
Specific contributions by partners		X
Partnership working processes	X	X
Staffing development	X	X
Accountability:		
a) to partners		X
b) to wider stakeholders	X	

Figure 6.2   Components of a PPP's business plan

The main board of a PPP is likely to be fairly large in statutory or voluntary based partnerships – for example it is clear from the 2002 Survey of Local Strategic Partnerships that the average size of a LSP board is fairly large; the boards of many voluntary based PPPs such as economic or learning partnerships are also likely to be reasonably large – for example the Kent and Medway Economic Board has 29 members (in mid-2004). While most of the partners will have only one representative on the board some of the key organizations (particularly local authorities) may have multiple individual representation. This is hardly surprising given that one of the aims of partnership working is inclusivity. Commercially based PPPs and those delivering specific services, on the other hand, are likely to have much smaller boards although there may be several representatives from each partner.

Any board with more than about half a dozen members needs careful management; it is just not practical to try and deal with every detail through a large board. Logic therefore suggests the creation of an executive committee of some sort but this approach immediately runs the risk of appearing to create an inner circle with all its implications of exclusivity which is directly contrary to the whole inclusive concept of partnership working. Thus the choice of who to appoint to an executive committee becomes political in nature. There appears to be four possible ways of approaching this, all of which are justifiable:

1. Involve the relevant 'office holders' if such posts exist (chair, vice chair, chairs of sub-groups and so on).

2. Invite the representatives of the core members.

3. Elect members from the full partnership board.

4. Appoint those perceived as being the key leaders in the partnership regardless of their constituency.

Option 2 runs the risk of disenfranchising the associate members while option 4 is very much the most difficult to adopt since it relies on subjective views rather than objectivity. Some PPPs appear to have adopted a good old-fashioned compromise by mixing options 2 and 3 or 2 and 4 – supplementing the core representatives with associate members or by coopting one or two well-recognized community leaders. A variation on this is to change the associate or coopted members on a regular, perhaps annual, basis.

Whatever method is adopted it is important that the resultant executive committee does not take over the role of the main partnership board. Its function should be limited to business management rather than policy development, although preliminary discussions in respect of the latter will obviously take place; in particular the executive committee is likely to be the forum which sanctions research into possible options, and which authorizes the partnership secretariat to have preliminary discussions with relevant stakeholders to seek their views. The aim of such considerations should be to propose options to the main board which have a realistic chance of being adopted rather than to determine policy as such. If handled properly (in accordance with agreed guidelines and with good briefing from the executive director) a well-run executive committee will be enormously beneficial to the success of a partnership. The ultimate test is whether the committee retains the confidence of the full partnership board.

CASE STUDIES: Structures to support a partnership board

One of the characteristics of partnership working is the desire for inclusivity. Inevitably this leads to fairly large boards and this, in turn, means that most PPPs have developed executive committees or specialist groups to support their board. The 2002 Local Strategic Partnership survey showed that 74 per cent of LSPs have an executive board of some sort (Table 11). Voluntary based partnerships are no different. The *Bedfordshire and Luton Economic Development Partnership* is currently reviewing its group structure prior to incorporation but is likely to support their formal board through an officer group which will meet monthly. The *Hampshire Economic Partnership* has an executive committee the chair of which sits on the main board, and operates through dedicated sector groups, a structure which is very similar to that adopted by the *Buckinghamshire Economic Partnership*. Some operate with slightly less formality – the *Kent and Medway Economic Board* prefers to retain its flexibility and responsiveness by not having any standing groups as such but creating ad hoc groups as required. The service delivery partnerships at both *Norfolk* and *Milton Keynes* are supported by monthly operational groups which resolve detailed operational matters, referring any strategic issues to the main board. Both operational groups are chaired by the client and have broadly equal representation from the client and contractor.

As far as the business of the board is concerned it needs to be recognized that the board itself is unlikely to be able to do everything or consider every issue in detail. Subgroups are therefore likely to be needed, whether to thrash out the details of a specific policy issue or to handle delivery details of a particular service. This immediately creates problems of membership and the degree of delegated freedom; the partner organizations are likely to have their own approaches to these problems which may well be very different from each other (for example a public authority usually has standing committees with specified freedom to act in certain areas while much of the private sector will act on a more ad hoc basis). As far as membership of subgroups is concerned there is always a tendency to invite the most vocal to serve (particularly in the case of larger strategically oriented PPPs) but a more justifiable approach is to try and ensure that the membership of a subgroup reflects the balance of the main board. The question of how much freedom of action to give subgroups is important since nothing is likely to irritate partners more if they contribute time and energy to the work of a subgroup only to see their conclusions overturned by a less well informed main board (particularly if, as is often the case, subgroup membership is their only chance of influencing the partnership). As with most PPP issues there can be no absolute answers since much will depend on circumstances but it is important that, when setting up subgroups, boards make clear decisions on their terms of reference and so on in order to avoid future problems.

At the more operational level PPPs will need to make a decision on how they will actually perform their duties, whether of a strategic or executive nature. There is a natural tendency to try and build up a partnership's own resources to perform these tasks (particularly if it has been decided to appoint a strong executive director who might be expecting a powerful support structure) but this approach should be treated with caution for three main reasons:

- Empire building in a partnership leads inevitably to conflict between the partnership and its partners.

- Cost – additional partnership staff lead to an ongoing increase in the fixed operating costs of the partnership.

- A partnership will generally need to have access to a wide range of expertise but not necessarily on a regular basis.

While clearly there is a need for a minimal level of staff to act as a secretariat for the partnership and support the work of particular project groups, it is sensible to resist any further increases beyond the minimal level. It is far more beneficial to make use of staff already employed by the individual partners or to engage consultants where necessary; this has a number of advantages:

- It encourages ownership of partnership activities by the staff of the partners; this is particularly important for the long-term success of the partnership.

- It widens the pool of specialist staff available to the partnership.

- It optimizes the use of resources.

Thus by using specialist staff in partners a partnership can both nurture the concept of partnership working and optimize the skills available to support its work at minimal cost without creating unnecessary tension between itself and the partners. This approach is predicated on the assumption that there is a good working relationship between a PPP and the partners and again highlights the need to ensure that the executive director has excellent inter-personal and political skills and has a good knowledge of the individual partners.

SUMMARY

- A key task of the chair and executive director is to develop a management style which fosters partners' confidence in the partnership.

- The operational arrangements of a PPP should be underpinned by the principles of clarity and balance.

- A PPP is the creature of the partners; its agenda should therefore be set after consultation with the partners and should not usurp their functions.

- It is important that the chair and executive director maintain constant, and close, contact with the individual partners.

- Prioritization of a partnership's business within the overall agenda is a valuable way of involving the members of the board in the partnership.

- Every PPP should have both a strategic plan and an annual business plan. The former should cover the partnership's overall objectives, an outline of how it intends to achieve those objectives, an indication of its resource requirements, an indication of how it intends to evolve and guidelines on how it plans to work with others.

- The annual business plan should cover the following elements: measurable outputs, research/assessment reports, finance, partner involvement, working practices, staff development and accountability.

- It is useful to have an executive committee and board subgroups provided there are clear procedures governing their membership and roles.

- Staffing levels in a PPP should be kept to a minimum; it is better from the point of view of both partnership commitment and use of resources to involve specialist staff in the partner organizations or consultants.

CHAPTER 7

Accountability and Keeping in Touch

The increase in the use of the word 'accountability' has been noticeable in the last few years; however the word has traditionally been used in two different ways in the public and private sectors. In the public sector accountability has always been viewed in a democratic sense – elected individuals are accountable to their electorate for the public services which their organization delivers. The private sector has tended to use the term in a more restricted, financial sense – a business is accountable for the funds which it manages and this accountability is demonstrated in the annual accounts that a company has to prepare.

Both these traditional distinctions have become much more blurred in the last few years. The public sector has had to become much more conscious of the financial dimension of their work; accountability in the financial sense is now much clearer, and is becoming more so as the proportion of services delivered through the contractual route increases. There is now a great deal more financial detail about public bodies and their activities available in the public domain and elected representatives can no longer escape their financial accountability responsibilities. Equally the private sector has come to acknowledge a greater degree of accountability to their shareholders; the major institutional investors have become much more involved in the way companies are managed and are increasingly flexing their muscles in the corporate environment. Other organizations in the education, voluntary and community sectors are also becoming much more conscious of the wider accountability basis which is emerging. This blurring of the traditional distinctions has had a consequential impact on the issue of accountability for PPPs. As we have seen, PPPs are a new type of organization – they are carrying out duties and delivering services for the benefit of the community, but are not public sector bodies with a clear line of democratic accountability through elected representatives.

It is often glibly said that a key precondition for the success of a PPP is the demonstration of accountability; indeed, during the establishment of a partnership, of whatever category, all the potential partners will undoubtedly support the concept without question. However when it becomes necessary to translate the concept into the realities of how a partnership will actually work it sometimes becomes difficult to reconcile the different approaches to accountability – partnership working makes it necessary to review the traditional concepts of accountability. While the position for each individual PPP will be specific for that PPP it is therefore useful for the partners to think through the principles of accountability at an early stage in a partnership's development in order to avoid confusion at a later stage.

TYPES OF ACCOUNTABILITY

In their report *Building Better Partnerships* (2001) the Commission on Public Private Partnerships, set up by the IPPR, attempted to bring together the various strands of accountability in the following definition:

> *Public accountability is a pre-condition for the legitimate use of public authority. It is the basis on which citizens are willing to delegate power to others to act on their behalf. Without proper accountability mechanisms organisations delivering services are not subject to democratic oversight and control, the rights of citizens are uncertain, and services are unlikely to reflect the needs of service users. Accountability is therefore an end as well as a means* (Page 231).

This definition is a useful starting point but it is worth exploring further the concept of accountability (insofar as it relates to PPPs) under four headings (as shown in Figure 7.1):

- political accountability
- managerial accountability
- legal and financial accountability
- community accountability.

The first half of this chapter deals with the concept of accountability under these headings. Linked to the issue of accountability is the question of how to communicate with partners and stakeholders – after all, a partnership can only demonstrate its accountability through a coherent communication programme; this is covered in the second half of the chapter.

POLITICAL ACCOUNTABILITY

The term 'political accountability' is used in the broadest sense in this section; it is taken to mean the accountability which each partner has to its own constituency – how a partner represents its own interests and reports back to its constituency on the results of that representation. Looked at in that way it immediately becomes clear that there are significant differences in the validity of the different sectors. Public bodies

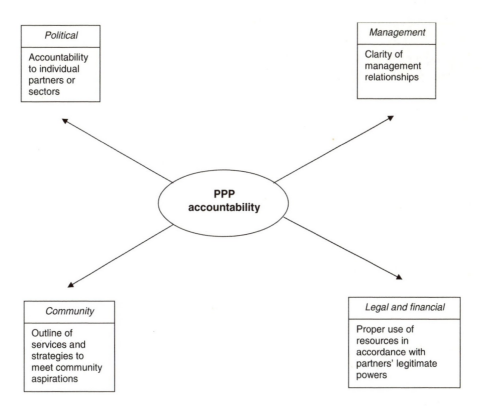

Figure 7.1 PPP accountability

are, in general, headed by directly elected representatives or by nominees, many of whom have come through an elective process of some sort. They can therefore trace their accountability roots, often to a manifesto of some sort. Public sector representatives are also accustomed to the practice of referring back and consulting their nominating bodies for guidance. This is not so easy for representatives from other sectors who will either come from a representative body (such as a chamber of commerce or umbrella voluntary organization) or from a specific organization (such as an individual company or educational body). In either case it is a moot point whether such representatives can really be said to be accountable to their wider constituency in the same way as elected members from the public sector.

The inevitable variations in the degree of individual accountability amongst the representatives on a PPP's board immediately raises the question of whether or not the PPP as a whole can really be said to be politically accountable (in the sense of this section). It is clearly unreasonable for anyone involved in establishing a PPP to impose democratic constraints on how partners should manage their own affairs; however it is reasonable to ask partners to be as open and democratic as possible in the way in which they nominate their representatives and in how those representatives consult their constituency. An example of this approach can be found in the way that the South East Regional Assembly (SEERA) operates. Like most regional assemblies SEERA has a mixed membership with, in its case, two-thirds from local authorities (democratically elected) and one-third from other organizations. The Assembly's standing orders ask, but do not demand, that the nominees from other organizations should be appointed in as open a manner as possible. While the Assembly cannot insist on this given the independent nature of the various non-local authority bodies it can at least present itself as having tried in a reasonable way to ensure that it is accountable to all its members. PPPs, however, do not have the same sort of devotion to constitutional niceties as a statutory body such as a regional assembly. They are therefore unlikely to be in a position to insist on nominating procedures (however much some of the public sector members may desire it) – indeed such insistence can be counter-productive. An interested and enthusiastic volunteer from any organization is worth more to a PPP than a reluctant representative elected on some sort of Buggins Turn principle.

The key question is whether the concept of political accountability (as defined here) actually matters in partnership working. The answer will probably be different depending on the nature of the PPP. Those partnerships at the strategic development end of the spectrum (whether statutory or voluntary based) will need to develop processes which maximize the opportunity to demonstrate accountability to the partners and wider community. It is unreasonable to expect that the non public sector partners should constantly seek to confirm their views with the individual members of their constituency; they should not have to justify every single one of their actions. However they can be asked to operate as openly and transparently as possible so that those they represent have ample opportunity to influence them. Partners in PPPs concerned with service delivery will be in a somewhat different position. They will be in the partnership because of their particular role to deliver, or contribute to the delivery of, a particular service. Their accountability can therefore be assessed by reference to the actual outputs of the partnership. However, because of the nature of partnership working, their political accountability will also have a second dimension, namely that of value for money.

MANAGERIAL ACCOUNTABILITY

In traditional organizations managerial accountability is usually fairly straightforward. Individuals report up the line to a relevant director who, in turn, reports to the chief executive and board structure. The position in a partnership structure is slightly different for two reasons:

- Executive action on behalf of a partnership is not always carried out by direct partnership employees; in some cases a partnership may not have any employees, or may only have a minimum staff (perhaps part time or secondees). Even where a partnership does have direct employees they will often be relying on colleagues in the partner organizations for some elements of the delivery process. The executive functions of a partnership may therefore be carried out in part by individuals with a divided line of accountability; however committed they may be to the concept of partnership, their background (and career development prospects) may inevitably temper the way in which they carry out their partnership duties.

- The ultimate authority in a partnership (the board) will be made up of representatives from different sectors. While it is easy to ask members of a board to set aside their partisan feelings when serving on the board, their fundamental loyalties will always be with their own constituency.

This inherent weakness of a partnership can only be overcome through strong leadership from the chair and executive director. It is their task to ensure that there is clarity over both the decision-making process at board level and the subsequent responsibilities for executive action. While on the face of it this is fairly obvious there are sometimes some difficult consequences – for example a transport partnership may decide on a particular policy in respect of say parking; at board level the council representatives may have acquiesced (perhaps reluctantly) in the broader interests of partnership working. The implications of the policy decision will have to be executed by council officers who may feel that their internal career prospects are being damaged by having to carry out partnership policy (as opposed to direct council policy). In this sort of situation it is incumbent on the chair or executive director to protect the interests of the individual officer – in other words there is a duty of care on the partnership leadership. Staff in partner organizations who experience this sort of support will be far more willing to carry out partnership decisions. The managerial accountability issue in contractually based service delivery partnerships is slightly different; the partners will have specific responsibilities under the terms of the contract and the staff employed by the individual partners will therefore be working specifically for the partnership. Indeed one of the benefits of such a partnership is that the individual staff member may have greater freedom of action than hitherto.

The essential thing is to ensure that there is clarity in the decision-making process backed up by a clear line of managerial responsibility. That line of responsibility will terminate with the chair which reinforces the need to ensure that the chair has the necessary local standing and confidence of the partners.

LEGAL AND FINANCIAL ACCOUNTABILITY

Successful partnership working is based on openness and transparency and nowhere is this more important than in the financial and legal area. All the partners and the wider community need to be reassured that partnership resources are being properly applied to support the partnership's activities and are not benefiting one or other particular partner. The private sector is sometimes uncomfortable with the degree of open book accounting which is familiar to the public sector but it is a price of partnership working that is both justifiable and has to be paid. Many PPPs, particularly those at the strategic end of the spectrum (such as most LSPs), will not need to concern themselves with legal or financial accountability issues. However, as we have seen, an increasing number of partnerships are being given delegated authority to either carry out action directly on behalf of the partners (such as the delivery of specific services) or to authorize others to carry out action on their behalf. This inevitably raises issues of legal and financial accountability.

Chapter 4 discussed the structural options open to a PPP and the issues of legal and financial accountability will be an important element in the consideration of which structure to adopt. The chapter pointed out that many partnerships will be happy to leave the legal and financial accountability with the individual partners; partners (such as councils, chambers of commerce, health trusts, individual companies and so on) will already have their own structures and procedures in place and it is often simpler to use them rather than to create new structures. Indeed, in some cases it may not be possible for a partnership to assume legal accountability for some activities even if they adopt a company structure – for example the Housing Corporation will only make grants to authorised recipients such as housing associations, and the European Union may require councils to be the accounting body for certain of their funds.

While this may appear to be a perfectly sensible approach it does raise some issues which need consideration at the outset. The internal processes of a partner acting on behalf of a partnership will need to be explained to the other partners who may feel that they are inappropriate or too onerous or restrictive – for example a university may insist that a fixed percentage of any contractual funds received should go towards its central costs; partner organizations may treat VAT differently and so on. It is important that all the partners accept at the outset the implications of asking one of their colleague partners to act on their behalf – it is no good complaining afterwards.

A second potential problem is the issue of what happens to any assets created by a partnership's activities but delivered for legal accountability reasons through a specific partner. In many cases this will not be an issue – physical assets such as a community facility or transport infrastructure will have a natural home for future ownership. However intangible assets such as an information database or coursework material are more difficult to assign. All the partners who came together to seek funds to develop such assets will wish to have subsequent free access to the material regardless of any restrictions which the recipient partner would normally have insisted upon. A council entering into a service delivery partnership with a private sector contractor will need to ensure that it retains access to, and control of, the data and procedures used by the contractor (albeit under conditions which might be specified by the latter). It follows that, when considering whether and how to invite a partner to accept legal and financial accountability on behalf of a partnership, it is essential to clarify the rights of the other partners before any negotiations are entered into with a third party. This simple objective is sometimes difficult to deliver – partners do not join a partnership with the intention of being obliged to compromise or amend their administrative procedures but to deliver desired objectives.

In this connection it is important for the credibility of partnership working that any legal and financial accountability arrangements that a partnership agrees with a partner acting on its behalf should be published more widely to the wider stakeholder group. A partnership must be seen to take responsibility for its actions even if it operates through a partner for legal reasons – it is only in this way that it can demonstrate the added value of partnership working.

The position is somewhat different where a PPP develops its own independent legal status and then enters into contracts with a third party. The partnership will need to develop its own internal systems to satisfy the usual legal and financial requirements of a company (such as an audit committee) and it is important to ensure that the individual core partners are content with such arrangements. As in the case where partners act on behalf of a partnership, the question of the ownership of assets created by the partnership needs careful consideration. There will probably be no problems while the partnership continues to exist in its original form but thought needs to be given as to what should happen if membership changes or the partnership is wound up. If new members who have not contributed to the creation of an asset join then should they have the same rights as the original members? Access to course material is a good example. This need not be an issue if it is thought through at the outset (in this example a joining fee might be appropriate). The disposal of assets (whether financial, physical or intellectual) on the winding up of a partnership operating under a company structure will need to be set out in the articles of association and reflected in the partnership's operating procedures. If the assets are to be distributed to the members (as opposed to being handed on to a similar organization) then there may be taxation implications.

If a partnership does decide to adopt its own legal persona then clearly it will have to publish and audit its accounts in the prescribed manner. Such accounts tend to be seen and approved by the board and then filed. While the full figures should always remain open to public inspection it is a useful practice to produce an edited or simplified version for formal submission to the governing bodies of the individual partners; this can then be used as a vehicle for a personal presentation by the chair or executive director to the partners. This has the merit of ensuring that there is at least a formal annual report to the partners, thus strengthening the accountability principle.

COMMUNITY ACCOUNTABILITY

Chapter 1 pointed out that the basic purpose of a PPP is to deliver 'desired policy outcomes that are in the public interest'. PPPs however are not governed by a directly elected board – members are drawn from the representatives of preformed constituencies. There is therefore no direct accountability line between a PPP and the individual members of the community. As we have already seen it can also be argued that some members of a partnership's board have limited accountability to their own constituency.

It therefore becomes difficult to see how a PPP can demonstrate accountability to the community as a whole notwithstanding the purpose quoted above. It is much easier to do this with those partnerships concerned with service delivery – there will be a published set of outcomes which can be linked to a specific sector of the community and community representatives (either via the council or directly elected) will often be on the partnership board. There is thus a direct accountability relationship between the partnership and the community.

Partnerships involved in strategic development are in a very different position. For a start there is the difficult issue of defining the term 'community'. First of all there is the geographic context. Although the geographic area covered by a PPP is generally easy to define, a strategy development partnership has to operate in a wider regional context – the economic, educational or health strategy of a community is inevitably closely linked to the surrounding communities. In order to give a wider context to their work some partnerships, particularly voluntary based partnerships such as economic or learning PPPs (which can adopt a fairly flexible approach to membership) encourage membership from adjacent areas (often on an associate or observer basis), while many partnerships of all types invite representation from an appropriate regional body.

Secondly there is the concept of 'community' itself; a community is broader than the local electorate – in addition to the latter in any given area there are those who live elsewhere but who commute in to work or use the recreational facilities, and there are those too young to work These individuals have every right to express an opinion on the work of a strategy development partnership but are difficult to categorize in membership terms.

The concept of community accountability is thus difficult to incorporate in partnership activity and it is only really in the last few years with the establishment of

Local Strategic Partnerships, with their specific task of developing a 'community strategy', that efforts have been made to do so. The 2002 Survey of LSPs showed the lengths to which LSPs have gone to try and cover the full breadth of community interests; Table 8 of that Survey listed 37 organizations or categories (some of which covered multiple organizations) nominating members of LSPs. The extent to which other PPPs will wish to involve wider community groups will depend on the nature of each partnership. What does seem clear however is the need to ensure that every PPP, of whatever type, should develop a wide range of communication tools to endeavour to publicize their activities to the wider community so that the latter can at least comment on a partnership's work.

The IPPR's Commission on Public Private Partnerships suggested that PPPs should base their approach to accountability on three principles:

- *Transparency*. Adopting and publishing the highest possible level of disclosure of the activities of a partnership.

- *Responsibility*. Defining clearly and publishing the responsibilities of the partnership and the individual partners.

- *Responsiveness*. Providing the opportunity for every member and sector of the community to respond to a partnership's work and reacting accordingly.

While these principles were developed with specific reference to strategic service delivery partnerships, they can be applied to the full range of PPPs.

KEEPING IN TOUCH

In the initial stages of a partnership's development, the chair, partnership champion and members of the steering group will become used to almost continuous communication – a partnership does not come into existence on a logical or linear basis; it emerges following numerous meetings and negotiations, both bilateral and multilateral, as potential partners work out their proposals and counter proposals to the suggestions put forward by others. This inevitably leads to an almost continuous communication process. Much of this is fairly informal via personal contact, although conclusions will all need to be written down and formalized at some point. There is therefore a natural inclination, once a partnership has been established, to pay less attention to communication and to concentrate more on getting things up and running.

While understandable, this tendency is dangerous and should be resisted – Figure 6.1, page 79 (the 'confidence curve') shows what everyone hopes will happen but this curve can be damaged (perhaps irreparably) if communication with the wider stakeholder group is not maintained at a high level. While the level and emphasis of a communication strategy will change as a partnership evolves there will always be four objectives to the strategy (which are interrelated and not mutually exclusive):

- the maintenance and encouragement of political support and goodwill for the partnership;

- the generation of adequate resources for the partnership;

- the optimization of the impact of the partnership by reporting successes and thus generating confidence in its proposals;

- the demonstration of the partnership's accountability.

As we have seen, every PPP has a wide range of stakeholders (see Figure 5.1, page 63); indeed some partnerships such as LSPs have an infinite range. These stakeholders are the ultimate recipients of a communication strategy. However the four objectives listed above are not equally important to all the stakeholders so each partnership needs to develop a strategy which is tailored to each audience segment. The following notes set out the main ways through which a partnership can keep in touch with its stakeholders and these are summarized in Figure 7.2.

PERSONAL CONTACT

PPPs, because they are a relatively new form of organization, require careful nurturing if they are to become successful and gain the confidence of their partners. As we have

Element	Primary Objective	Primary Target Audience
Personal contact • by chair • by executive director	Political support Resources	Governing bodies of partners Officers of partners
Quarterly reports	Confidence building through successes	Partners
Annual reports	Accountability and political support	All partners and stakeholders
Newsletters and websites	Confidence building	All partners and stakeholders
Public meetings and themed seminars	Confidence building and accountability	All partners and stakeholders

Figure 7.2   Elements of a communication strategy

seen, the initial stages of a partnership's development rely to a considerable extent on the personal skills of the partnership champion and chair; the longer-term strength of a partnership relies in a similar way on the continuing personal contacts between a partnership's leadership and the partners.

The chair of a partnership is a pivotal figure and must be respected by all the partners; it is likely that the chair will also be a member of the governing body of at least some of the partners – he or she may be a councillor, a board member of the chamber of commerce, or a member of the health trust board. It is pertinent to note that the local council leader chaired just over half of the LSPs surveyed in 2002 (Table 10 of the Survey). The chair will therefore be in an excellent position to promote the work of a partnership in a wide range of both formal and informal ways. The key objective of this type of contact by the chair is to maintain and encourage political support for the partnership; ideally the chair should not be engaged in the details of resource negotiations or gaining support for a particular project – the chair is there to build up a feeling of confidence in the partnership's work.

The role of the executive director is slightly different. While the executive director will obviously have many opportunities to promote the work of the partnership in a general or strategic sense, much of their time will be spent on converting that general level of support to specific support in resource or project terms. The executive director is likely to have closer contact with the relevant officers in the partner organizations (note comments in Chapter 2 on the value of an officer group in developing a PPP) who are key players in the resource game rather than with the individual board members of the partners.

The above general comments on the importance of maintaining a network of contacts by the chair and executive director are fairly obvious and reflect what goes on in every large organization. However it is worth stressing a few supplementary points which relate specifically to a partnership's communications strategy. It is important that the chair and executive director maintain close liaison on the message they wish to impart and on their respective diary commitments. A partnership's work generally cuts across a number of agendas – it tends to be multi-disciplinary in approach (even service delivery partnerships usually cover more than one area of activity) whereas the partners tend to be organized on a departmental structure based around single functions. There is therefore a danger that a proposal or idea from a partnership, while it may chime precisely with one part of say a council, may be seen as threatening to another. Thus careful liaison is needed between the chair and executive director to ensure that a consistent approach is always being expressed; careful diary management also makes it possible for either the chair or executive director to prepare the way for the other when putting forward a proposal so that the optimum result can be achieved.

Essentially it is about managing the process of personal contacts; this need to develop a coordinated approach between the chair and executive director emphasizes yet again the need to develop a strong leadership function for a partnership based on compatibility and complementarity between the two individuals.

FORMAL REPORTS TO PARTNERS

There is a tendency to assume that the board members of a partnership will automatically report back to their constituent bodies to keep them informed of the partnership's activities. Unfortunately experience has shown that this is not always the case – some board members are diligent about this task, while others assume that the secretariat will do so; others just don't see it as part of their role. It is therefore helpful to supplement the informal personal contact outlined above with brief written reports submitted on a regular basis (say quarterly) by the executive director to the individual governing bodies of the partners. The report need not be overlong – after all a partnership does not want to have its discussions replayed at the boards of all the individual partners – but it needs to be the same for all partners. The main purpose of such a report is to emphasize the successes that have been achieved and to demonstrate the added value of the partnership. For example a learning partnership can use the report to demonstrate to each of the partner institutions how the partnership has been able to say strengthen their curriculum or broaden their appeal. If possible it is helpful if the executive director can present this report in person to each partner rather than leave it to the latter's staff; this ensures consistency of message and also enhances the visibility of the executive director.

Quarterly reports will need to be supplemented by formal annual reports. While every PPP will be different in the degree of detail and so on which is included, the annual report should give relevant financial information. The latter should include both the partnership's direct income and expenditure (including programme funds) and that incurred by partners on behalf of the partnership. It is only in this way that the full scale of the partnership's activities can be shown. The aim of the annual report is twofold – to demonstrate the added value of the partnership, and to strengthen its accountability to the partners and wider community.

NEWSLETTERS AND WEBSITES

Newsletters are a valuable way of reaching a much wider audience. Today's technology means that as many newsletters are produced and circulated electronically as are printed and circulated through the postal system. The former has the advantage of speed and cost but is restricted to a mailing list, while a printed report has the advantage of presenting a better public image and potentially reaching a wider audience. The choice of which method to use will depend upon the nature of the PPP and the objective of the communication. Newsletters do not lend themselves to the

CASE STUDIES: Maintaining accountability and keeping in touch

As the main text makes clear, the issue of accountability is a difficult one for definitional reasons. Financial accountability is fairly straightforward with many PPPs using the relevant statutory authority where appropriate. Democratic accountability, in the broadest sense, is a different matter. Some partnerships, such as the *Hampshire Economic Partnership*, specifically expect their board members (or sector representatives in the case of Hampshire) to formally report back to their constituencies; *Hackney Borough Council*, in the terms of reference which they issue to members of the *Hackney Strategic Partnership*, state explicitly that 'members will need to ... cascade information down to their sector and organization'. Most partnerships, such as the *Buckinghamshire Economic Partnership*, require their director to make quarterly reports to the board and some then invite their board members to forward the report to their own organization. On a wider accountability basis some partnerships hold regular open meetings – the *Northamptonshire Partnership* holds two per annum, one of which acts as an AGM. The *South East Climate Change Partnership* holds an annual open forum for all interested stakeholders. Newsletters of some sort are another regular way of communicating with stakeholders – the Kent and *Medway Economic Board* publishes a newsletter twice a year and issues reports on each seminar or event which they run, while the *Portsmouth and South East Hants Partnership* publishes occasional newsletters. The *Buckinghamshire Economic Partnership* sends regular emails to a mailing list of about 200 leaders within the county to keep them informed. Most partnerships have their own websites and these are growing increasingly valuable both for publishing information and encouraging feedback; some of these however are incorporated within the relevant local authority's site which reduces their effectiveness. On a more operational level the *Milton Keynes Support Services Partnership* made a point of maintaining contact with both the unions (through regular meetings) and the staff involved throughout the process of developing the partnership. In their 2001 Survey of Strategic Partnerships, the New Local Government Network (NLGN) commented 'It is important to keep control of the communication process and not to leave it to others to spread the news, and to ensure that rumour is not allowed to gain ground. *Sheffield* [which established a partnership to deliver IT and financial services] had a hot line updated daily.'

seeking of specific support for particular projects; they really exist to generate a feeling that the partnership is of value to the wider community and that therefore its initiatives should be taken seriously.

Websites are a variety of newsletter but with some significant differences. The information is available to a much wider audience but there is the problem of ensuring that the material is up to date (which has a cost implication). Many partnerships appear to have compromised by restricting their website to a fact sheet, with some major highlights of the previous twelve months or so, and giving a contact point for further information.

PUBLIC MEETING AND SEMINARS

Most of the comments in the previous sections will be very familiar to anyone involved in developing a communications strategy for any large organization. Public meetings are also very familiar to public sector bodies, while the private sector is used to holding AGMs in public. PPPs, however, because of their unusual nature, have the opportunity to develop a more hybrid style of meeting. In addition to using public meetings to promote their activities and demonstrate their value (the traditional objective of such meetings), PPPs can use the meetings to generate active feedback from the wider community in order to demonstrate their accountability.

Many partnerships (particularly LSPs) have therefore started to promote public seminar type events; these are open to the wider public and are often organized around a particular theme to encourage public participation. While LSPs have probably led the way in this area of activity, many economic and learning partnerships also promote regular seminars of this nature. The organization of such events needs care – the audience needs to feel that their views will count and that it will be a genuinely participative process; thus a feedback system needs to be considered. The approach most commonly adopted is to circulate a report of the event with consequential action to the audience (either by post or electronically). The electronic approach, which is gaining in popularity, has the advantage of initiating a dialogue which can be linked to a partnership's website. This combination of open meetings and electronic follow-up has the potential to become an extremely valuable communication tool for PPPs.

OPERATIONAL COMMUNICATIONS

The comments in the previous sections relate specifically to managing communications between a partnership and the wider stakeholder group. Of equal importance is the maintenance of good communications within the operational dimensions of a partnership. Most PPPs are fairly small organizations (although some service delivery partnerships can be large) and there can be a danger of assuming that everyone involved knows what is going on. It is important that the executive director takes the time to talk to those involved at the 'sharp end' both to keep them fully informed but also to pick up any early signals of possible problems arising from the unusual nature of partnership working. PPPs are very much at the learning end of the organizational spectrum and it is well worth spending time on seeking internal feedback.

SUMMARY

- It is important to clarify at the outset what each partner understands by the concept of accountability, and to agree on how a partnership will fulfil its accountability duties.

- It is useful to analyse a PPP's accountability under four headings: political, managerial, legal and financial, and community.

- Political accountability is difficult to achieve in some cases; the objective should be to try and ensure that all members of every partner's constituency have the opportunity to influence the partnership.

- Strong partnership leadership is necessary in order to ensure clarity in a partnership's decision-making processes backed up by clear lines of managerial responsibility.

- It is essential to clarify the conditions under which a partner enters into contractual arrangements on behalf of a partnership with a third party.

- The long-term ownership of any assets created by a partnership needs to be clarified at the outset.

- Community accountability is difficult to achieve given the difficulty of defining the term community and of determining how to involve the full range of community interests.

- A communications strategy for a partnership is essential in order to maintain political support, generate adequate resources, create confidence in its activities and demonstrate accountability.

- Continuous personal contact by the chair and executive director with all partners (which should be coordinated in terms of both the message and timing) is an essential element of any communications strategy.

- It cannot be assumed that board members will report back regularly to their constituency; the executive director should take the lead in submitting a regular quarterly report, supplemented by a formal annual report.

- Newsletters and websites are a useful means of communicating successes but need to be assessed carefully in terms of value for money.

- Public meetings and themed seminars are a valuable way of giving the wider community a chance to influence a partnership.

- Maintain a regular dialogue with those directly involved in the work of the partnership to ensure that the organization continues to learn how to improve.

CHAPTER 8

Setting Targets and Measuring Success

Public private partnerships are a relatively new type of organization; as we have seen this means that they will need fairly careful nurturing if they are to be successful. But it is important to know how successful they have been and this can only be achieved through setting targets and measuring how well a partnership succeeds in meeting those targets.

Traditional organizations have always been used to the concept of achieving an overall objective through meeting specific targets. However there have been significant differences between the way that the public and private sectors have approached the issue of targets, although these differences are now narrowing. The private sector, because it is funded through risk capital of some sort which expects a return on its investment, has always been very comfortable with the concept of adopting quantifiable targets and linking these to a financial return; companies are therefore accustomed to expressing numerical targets in all areas of their activities and to making use of those targets to manage the individual elements of their business. The increasing interest in a company's contribution to the environment and community as a whole has also meant that many businesses have become accustomed to setting wider goals, quantifying these where possible (for example devoting a certain proportion of profits to charitable activities or permitting individuals to undertake a specific number of days working on community projects). Target setting is not therefore an issue for the private sector, but this has not been true of the public sector until relatively recently.

In the public sector, targets have traditionally been related to the nature of the services delivered and to more general objectives such as improving the well-being of particular sectors of the community; often these were not expressed in numerical terms and only rarely in financial terms. However in the last twenty years or so public bodies have been obliged to provide a much closer link between targets and their financial consequences – a key component behind the making of policy choices is now value for money. This has had a consequential impact on the choice of more specific targets by public sector organizations, perhaps best demonstrated through the Government's Next Steps programme launched in the late 1980s. Under this programme many central government functions have been transferred to agencies which, in return for greater managerial freedom, have been obliged to accept a myriad of targets. This same process has been adopted for other public bodies such as local authorities, education or health bodies. Today central government funds are often tied to the achievement of specific targets. As a result service delivery targets are now often accompanied by unit cost targets. While many would argue that there are too many targets, and that these have led to micro-management of the public sector, there is no doubt that organizations in that sector are becoming more familiar with the idea of quantifiable targets while still retaining the softer 'community benefit' type of targets of the past. This evolution of approach in the public sector has made it much easier to set targets for hybrid bodies such as PPPs.

AIM OF TARGET-SETTING PROCESS

The overall aim of setting targets for a PPP is to provide clarity for the work of the partnership and to give a framework for managing the expectations of the partners. A partnership cannot do everything; it operates at the behest of the partners. The process of setting targets, which is integrated with the business planning process, is the mechanism through which the individual partners can quantify their hopes for the partnership's activity; it is the forum where the individual partners can 'trade off' their aspirations with each other. For example a PPP dealing with the development of the local health strategy will need to agree on specific targets for various health categories; 'consumer' or 'community' partners are likely to want to adopt fairly stretching targets while the health practitioners (who may well support such aspirations in idealistic policy terms) will be keen to stress the resource implications of the choices between the various options.

The process of managing the expectations of the individual partners through target setting will also help the clarity issue – what targets will become the specific responsibility of the partnership as opposed to the individual partners? There is an inevitable tendency for partners to propose, or be willing to agree to, a target which meets their expectations on the assumption that another partner will actually deliver the target. If the target suddenly becomes their responsibility their expectations may well become more realistic. Thus the target negotiation process must be closely linked to clarification of the delivery mechanism and built into the annual business planning process.

Within the overall aim of the target setting process will be two subsidiary objectives:

- the achievement of the partnership's long-term objectives;
- the achievement of acceptable performance standards.

The partnership process is essentially a long-term one and the *long-term objectives* of a PPP will be set out in the partnership's terms of reference or, in the case of a contractually based partnership, in the original contract and reflected in the strategic plan. These long-term objectives need to be broken down into realistic annual targets which may well require fairly difficult negotiations at the partnership board.

Performance standards in this context means the process by which outputs are delivered rather than the actual outputs themselves and have an important role to play in the target-setting process. Many PPPs, particularly those concerned with the delivery of services, are primarily established to improve the relevant performance standards by levering in additional resources or by introducing different managerial approaches or structures. It follows that targets for PPPs will usually include a gradually rising set of performance standards – partnership targets must reflect continuous improvement in the standards of service offered to the community if the partnership is to continue to offer added value and thus retain the confidence of partners.

TARGET SETTING APPLIED TO PPPs

Much of the above brief comments are generic in nature in that they can apply to the target-setting process for any organization. Target setting for PPPs, because of their unusual nature, has a number of specific differences with the target-setting process for their partners. The differences stem from two contrasting but related features of the two types of organization – timescale and accountability.

As far as *timescale* is concerned a partnership is established to achieve long-term change (whether in strategic terms or in terms of the nature of the services to be delivered); the individual partners, while clearly also having long-term goals, are focused on meeting shorter-term objectives – their performance is judged on a much more immediate basis.

Their *accountability* is also much more immediate – they are directly accountable to the electors, their members (in the case of a chamber of commerce) or to their shareholders. A partnership's accountability on the other hand is more indirect via the partners. It follows that, as a result of these differences, a partnership needs to have a much more robust long-term strategic plan, with clearly quantified targets, than the partners who can express their strategic goals in rather more general terms. A partnership can also afford to be slightly more relaxed over its short-term targets (provided they are consistent with the long-term strategy).

Against this overall contextual difference there are four particular areas where the nature of partnership working will affect the target-setting process.

OUTCOMES AND OUTPUTS

Whether of a strategic development or service delivery nature, PPPs are established to achieve long-term objectives – they are not set up to deliver a 'quick fix'. These objectives are set out in the strategic plan and are the *outcomes* which the partnership is aiming to deliver. These will be achieved by delivering certain specific tasks (the *outputs*) each year, either directly or through others, as set out in the annual business plan. The measurement of the achievement of the tasks (such as the provision of a particular type or range of training courses in the case of a lifelong-learning partnership) is fairly straightforward, as can be the unit cost. It is much more difficult to measure how that task has contributed to the overall outcomes for which the partnership was established – for example the course(s) in question might have been designed to improve the long-term recruitment prospects of the local economy. The latter will probably be difficult to quantify on an annual basis but can only really be assessed through, for example, surveying employers every few years.

This illustrates the difficulty of setting and assessing the strategic outcomes of a partnership's work, but it is essential that it should be done since the partnership will be judged on its long-term achievements. It is also important that a partnership's planning and reporting process, which will inevitably be built round an annual cycle, needs to be supplemented by regular reports on how the annual outputs have contributed to the achievement of the desired outcomes – it is only in this way that the real benefits of partnership working can be measured.

TIMESCALE FOR OUTPUT TARGETS

Because of their innovative nature, partnerships require a lot of learning from the partners – they will take time to appreciate the value of partnership working and to develop confidence in each other. They are unlikely (or unwilling) to make many changes in their attitudes or processes in the first few years of a partnership's existence. It is therefore unrealistic to set over-demanding output targets in the initial years – not only is there the danger that they may not be met but the consequences of not doing so may damage confidence in the partnership's ability to deliver. This is not to say that the targets should not be reasonable but it is sensible to adopt a gradually stretching set of output targets rather than to be over-ambitious in the short term.

PROCESS MANAGEMENT TARGETS IN PARTNERS

One of the principal reasons that a partnership is established is to improve the process by which local decisions are made or implemented. If a partnership is successful then there should be an impact on the decision-making process or operational processes of the individual partners. For example a Local Strategic Partnership will develop and regularly update the local community strategy; it will do this by drawing on and synthesizing the strategic work of both the various local partners and other local partnerships. It follows that the strategic development work undertaken by the latter bodies should therefore evolve to take account of the new relationship with the LSP. Recognition of this point may well be fairly uncomfortable for the individual partners (particularly for the members of the partners who are not directly personally involved in the partnership itself). Nevertheless this evolutionary process needs to be reflected in the annual targets set not only by the LSP (which, of course, will need to be accepted by the partner representatives on the LSP board) but also by the partners themselves. Process-change targets of this nature are undoubtedly difficult to both set and achieve because they effectively interfere with the internal management systems of other organizations – in a sense however they go to the heart of partnership working; if it is to be effective it will have a measurable impact on how the autonomous partner bodies manage their own business.

VALUE FOR MONEY

All the foregoing comments come together under the heading of value for money. A PPP will only prosper if it can show to the partners that, as a result of its existence, it has provided value for money – it has added value to the activities of each of the partners. Figure 8.1 illustrates the way that value for money is achieved through partnership working.

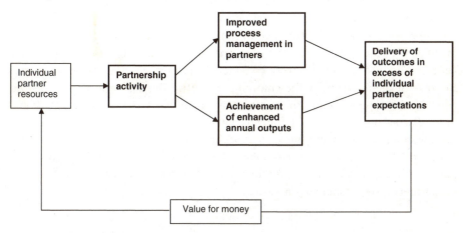

Figure 8.1   PPP value for money

The process of target setting, and the choice of targets as a result of that process, should be directly related to the four bold boxes of this diagram. All the targets should measure items which fit within one of these four boxes. In this way a partnership's targets will demonstrate its value for money which, in turn, will provide a strong foundation for the further collaboration in the long term.

CASE STUDIES: Establishing targets and measuring success

As indicated in the main text, setting targets for service delivery partnerships is fairly straightforward – for example *Working Links*, a joint venture between the Employment Service and a number of private sector contractors, operates nine of the government's Employment Action Zones. It is paid according to output-related targets (mainly the design and delivery of specific training courses) but receives additional funding if those attending courses are placed in a job, with a further bonus if the job lasts more than 13 weeks (that is, achieving an outcome). Targets for voluntary based partnerships tend to be less specific although EMDA has instituted a triennial review of its funding of partnerships (such as the *Northamptonshire Partnership*) to be assessed against the achievement of specific targets arising from the Regional Economic Strategy. Many other partnerships operate in the same way as the *Hampshire Economic Partnership* which sets specific targets in its annual business plan and which are the subject of a formal report and review every quarter.

Setting partnership targets is likely to be a fairly delicate matter. For this reason they cannot be left to chance and allowed to evolve in a somewhat ad hoc manner (or equally, dismissed because they are too difficult). It is interesting to note that, despite the obvious difficulty of setting targets for partnerships involved in strategy development, the 2002 Survey of Local Strategic Partnerships reported that 19 per cent of LSPs had already agreed to and set performance targets of some sort and that 62 per cent of those with no targets were considering doing so (Table 22 of the Survey). Because of their sensitivity the chair and executive director will need to devote considerable time and effort to the target-setting process – it requires more than a quick discussion at board level. It needs detailed bilateral discussions between the partnership leadership and the leaders of the core partners. In many ways it is an annual reaffirmation of the process which the chair of the initial steering group and partnership champion will have undertaken with potential partners at the outset of the partnership development process.

CHARACTERISTICS OF TARGETS

Each partnership will wish to set its own targets to suit its own particular requirements (and the requirements of its partners). However it is worth bearing in mind that all targets should have the following characteristics (see Figure 8.2):

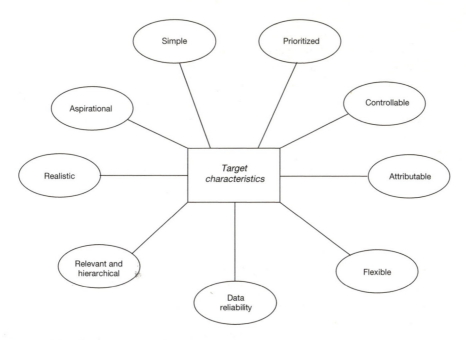

Figure 8.2   Characteristics of targets

Relevant and hierarchical

Targets must be clearly relevant to the partnership's work and should mesh with the targets adopted by partner organizations (and any wider context, such as regional targets). There needs to be a clear relationship between a partnership's targets and the wider world. For example, in the health, education and economic fields there are national targets; these are often broken down regionally and will need to be reflected in the local PPP's strategy. In turn the relevant local delivery agencies (partners) will need to adopt targets to match the partnership strategy.

Realistic

Targets must be realistic if they are to be taken seriously. Unrealistic or impractical targets are disregarded and are of no value – indeed they can become a distraction.

Aspirational

The counterpoint of realism is motivation. While it is important that a target should be realistic and seen to be achievable it is equally important that it should be set high enough to motivate the aspirations of the partners. Achieving the correct balance between realism and aspiration can sometimes be very difficult; the local political environment (from the consumer partners) will often be in conflict with the resource environment (the provider partners).

Simple

Targets should be simple and easy to understand. If an explanatory paragraph is needed then probably that target should be excluded. In this connection it is important to remember the audience for targets – in addition to the partners (who should have a reasonable idea of what a particular target means and why it has been chosen) the wider stakeholder group will also be keenly interested in a partnership's progress. It is therefore important that they understand the targets.

Prioritized

One of the lessons learnt from the Next Steps process was the importance of prioritizing targets. When the programme was initiated there was an understandable inclination to create a fairly large number of targets, some of which appeared to conflict with each other. It rapidly became necessary to identify a few key targets for each agency, a point which was re-emphasized in the 2003 Treasury *Guide to Setting Key Targets for Executive Agencies*. However it appears that the need to prioritize key targets has not been universally adopted across the public sector with many organizations either setting or being forced to set an increasing number of targets. Given the relative immaturity of PPPs and their general lack of resources it is counter-productive to adopt too many targets; a few key targets is a more valuable approach.

Flexible

It is important that targets are not seen as a straightjacket – circumstances will change and a partnership and the partners need to be prepared to change or amend a target if that seems reasonable. Hopefully this will not happen with strategic outcome targets but annual output targets may need adjustment. Occasionally it is possible to couch a target in conditional terms – for example to achieve an economic growth rate of x per cent provided the UK economy grows by y per cent.

Controllable

A target is only valuable if its achievement is perceived to be within the control of the partnership or partners. A house building target is of no value if there is no representative of the house building sector around the table. It is therefore important not to adopt a target the achievement of which depends upon the action of others (unless of course it is expressed in a conditional manner).

Attributable

The achievement of a target must be specifically attributed, whether to an organization or perhaps to an individual. Where a PPP has a legal entity or direct control of the resources then it is reasonable to attribute responsibility to the partnership as a whole. It is more usual, however, for the achievement of a target to be down to a specific partner, perhaps helped by others. For example an economic partnership might set a target for inward investment, the achievement of which might be the responsibility of a dedicated agency working with others. However such a target should only be set with the full support of the inward investment agency itself – it cannot just be imposed on them. Where a group of organizations is being asked to deliver a particular target then it is useful to ask one of those organizations to take the lead to ensure that the target is met. This point is fairly obvious and sounds simple but can be a real test of partnership working.

Data reliability

It is essential that targets are underpinned by reliable data accepted by all the partners; it is also extremely useful if the data is drawn from existing sources since it will then be unnecessary for the partnership to develop its own data collection systems. Not only is the latter approach a costly exercise but the validity might well be challenged by the partners. There are three aspects to the data issue:

- The raw data must be objectively measurable and accurate.

- The data must be compatible with the data used (and recognized) by the partners; in this connection it is important to ensure that common definitions are used – for example housing completions must be measured in the same way by all the partners in a housing-related PPP.

- There must be as much continuity as possible in the data and definitions. A partnership is aiming to deliver improved services or standards over time so changing databases or definitions is to be avoided. This is not always possible given the way in which politicians at both the national and local level tend to amend definitions to suit their own purposes.

TARGET REPORTING SYSTEM

It is of little value to spend time and effort on developing a robust system of targets unless it is underpinned by a regular reporting system which is taken seriously by the partnership board. Unfortunately this is often a function which tends to be overlooked by partnership managers since it can take time and detracts from activities such as launching new initiatives or widening a partnership's influence (activities which are much more attractive to undertake). Regular reporting on targets is an activity which should come high on the agenda of a partnership – indeed the New Local Government Network's Report on Service Delivery Partnerships in 2001 stressed the importance of ensuring that there is a formal performance reporting system for such partnerships.

STRATEGIC OR OUTCOME TARGETS

These will be set out in a PPP's strategic plan. Such outcomes will have to be measurable – a general objective to say 'improve the health of the community' is of no value in itself; it has to be measured by, for instance, mortality rates of certain major diseases. However one of the problems of adopting these sorts of outcomes is the difficulty of accessing timely data – much of the data likely to be useful in supporting broad objectives will probably be collected on a national basis, may not be annual and is likely to be published too late to be useful. For this reason it can be worthwhile to measure outcomes through the use of surveys. For example councils often carry out regular surveys to measure the effectiveness of their services and these can be used as a vehicle for adding specific questions to seek particular data to support the work of local partnerships (on commuting patterns, educational standards and so on). Chambers of commerce also carry out regular surveys which can be used in the same way. If surveys are used in this way it is essential that there is consistency in the methodology and questions asked in order to ensure that the resultant trend lines are sufficiently robust.

While extremely useful, surveys are not necessarily an annual occurrence. Another approach to measuring outcomes is to select specific statistics which are perceived as contributing to an outcome (preferably those which are already collected by a local agency) and plot them on a trend basis. Such figures should be treated with caution since they are likely to be raw data and collected for internal purposes only. However a way round this is to convert the annual figure into a three-year moving average; this helps to smooth out inconsistencies but will still give an overall trend.

Once outcome targets have been identified it is incumbent on the executive director to ensure that a regular reporting timetable is introduced and adhered to. Outcome trends are only likely to be reported on an annual basis (and sometimes less frequently) and they therefore lend themselves to publication at a partnership's annual meeting which is usually attended by a wide range of stakeholders. The reporting process thus becomes an integral element in the demonstration of a partnership's accountability to the wider community.

ANNUAL OUTPUT TARGETS

The measurement and publication of annual output targets, because they are much more specific in nature and generally attributable to a specific body (such as an inward investment agency), are easier to manage. If carefully chosen they can be the same as or directly aligned to the operational targets adopted by the individual partners. This means that there will be existing systems available to collect the data and it becomes a much simpler task for the executive director of the partnership to collate the data for the board. Quarterly reporting of such statistics should be possible but this requires positive action by the executive director based on a close working relationship with officer colleagues from the partner organizations. Annual output targets for service delivery PPPs are relatively easy to collect – indeed they may well be set out in the underlying contractual agreement with the financial arrangements dependent upon achieving the targets. Output targets are more difficult to set for partnerships who are more involved in the process of strategy development. Publication and adoption dates for particular strategies can be set but responsibility for implementation (usually at partner level) is likely to depend on resources or other external constraints. Targets relating to improvements in the process management of partners to support the development of partnership working can also be difficult to set but are worth attempting. The chair and executive director will need to exercise considerable diplomacy before proposing targets in the latter category.

The collection and publication of achievement against annual targets is only one part of the process; action will need to follow. Hopefully, in the majority of cases, achievement will closely follow targets so there will be no need to propose new strategies or operational changes. However this will not always be the case and the partnership board may need to review the position. There is a danger that, at this point, the other partners may be tempted to criticize or even attack the performance of the partner responsible. While understandable (particularly in the climate of local 'point scoring' so beloved of the media) this temptation should be resisted if possible – the concept of partnership working is based on mutual support and partners should be endeavouring to help each other achieve the target in question. This process of mutual support may need to be actively fostered by the chair – yet another reason why the latter needs to be an individual who enjoys the confidence of all the partners.

SUMMARY

- It is important to introduce systems by which a partnership's progress can be measured.

- The target-setting process provides clarity for work of a partnership and enables the expectations of the individual partners to be managed.

- Strategic outcome targets should be set out in a partnership's strategic plan and should be reported on at an annual meeting open to all the stakeholders.

- A useful way of measuring an outcome target is through regular surveys (provided they are robust and consistent); an alternative is to develop trend lines using local data.

- Annual output targets should be part of the annual business planning process and should tie in with long-term outcome targets (set in a partnership's strategic plan). They should be reported on a quarterly basis if possible.

- Targets should cover both the activities of the partnership and the performance management processes of the partners (to help assess their commitment to partnership working).

- Targets are the quantification of the goal of continuous improvement which every partnership should be setting out to achieve.

- There are nine characteristics of robust targets; they should be relevant and hierarchical, realistic, aspirational, simple, prioritized, flexible, controllable, attributable, and backed up by reliable data.

- Partners should be encouraged to support and offer help to colleague partners who fail to meet a target; fostering this attitude is an important aspect of the chair's role.

CHAPTER 9

Characteristics of Successful Partnerships

While public private partnerships have been in existence for some time (particularly contractually based partnerships), the full range and variety of PPPs has only really started to take shape in the last few years. It might therefore be regarded as presumptuous to try and identify what makes a successful partnership – indeed what is success in this context? The 2002 Survey of Local Strategic Partnerships did not attempt to identify success as such but identified issues which still needed to be resolved (the most important of which was 'developing wider and successful community engagement' – page 30), but the New Local Government Network's 2001 Report on Strategic Delivery Partnerships (which were, in effect, in the vanguard of the PPP movement) stated that 'the initial assessment is positive … Most of the cases studied had delivered significant service improvements' (page 8). It is therefore clear that some partnerships appear to have stronger foundations than others and that some parts of the country are embracing the partnership culture more enthusiastically than others; furthermore there do seem to be some features common to all the more successful partnerships of whatever category. Not all the partnerships display all of these features.

As we have seen every partnership is different – even within the same category of partnership there are significant differences; for example a Local Strategic Partnership in one area may have a completely different membership and modus operandi from a neighbouring LSP, while there are a tremendous variety of service delivery partnerships. Furthermore every partnership will have their own particular objectives – for example each economic partnership will set objectives appropriate to their own situation. These differences, coupled with the fact that we are still in the relatively early stages of the PPP movement, mean that it is difficult to adopt an objective test of success; however some partnerships clearly regard themselves as being on the right track.

PPPs are strategic in nature – they are established to achieve long-term objectives. As we have seen in Chapter 1 their primary aim is to deliver change for the benefit of the community; a secondary aim is to introduce a fundamental culture change in how public policy and services are developed and managed. They are therefore a new type of organization the success of which will only become apparent over the next couple of decades. In analysing the achievements of PPPs to date it appears that the reasons for their success can be categorized under four main headings:

- purpose and objectives
- leadership quality
- partnership values
- operational and management structures.

PURPOSE AND OBJECTIVES

No organization, particularly a new organization, can hope to succeed unless it has a clear purpose and objectives – you must know where you are going; in a sense a PPP has to be clearer about this than the more traditional organizations which make up their membership since the latter have to be persuaded to allocate resources and transfer some of their responsibilities to the partnership. There appear to be three elements to this.

CLEAR STRATEGIC OBJECTIVES

This is a fundamental precondition for success. Imprecise objectives are a recipe for failure. A PPP needs a very clear idea of the outcomes which it hopes to achieve over the next 5–10 years. Such outcomes must be understood and supported by all the partners if their commitment is to be secured. It is of course easier to do this for some partnerships than others – service delivery partnerships can usually set out their objectives with much greater clarity than those involved in strategy development. However the latter type of partnership can develop a clear vision of the future and can identify how to measure that vision (how the community would recognize the achievement of the vision – for example the number and type of jobs or houses, the range of educational opportunities, specific health characteristics). Successful partnerships need to spend a considerable amount of time at the outset in developing clarity of purpose; they should also not be afraid to revisit that discussion from time to time in order to refresh or retune the original objectives.

SPECIFIC ADDED VALUE

A PPP is a creature of the partners; it cannot therefore have a life of its own or try and impose its views on the partners. It has to be built from the bottom up and can only exist if it can demonstrate specific added value to the individual partners. A partnership must continuously show to the partners that it is enhancing their work through its existence. In parallel with this a partnership must also demonstrate that its existence does not threaten any of the partners – a successful partnership does not work in a hierarchical way but in collaboration, respecting the strengths of and contribution from each partner.

LONG-TERM PARTNER COMMITMENT

Because a PPP is concerned with the achievement of long-term change it is essential that the partners give the partnership their long-term commitment and support. Equally of course, commitment of this nature has to be earned by a partnership – it cannot be assumed – but it must be there. In particular it has to exist at both the political and administrative (officer) level. This presents an immediate challenge to the governing structures of all the individual partners (not just to local authorities) which have to accept that successful partnership working requires a culture change in the way that their organization works; they have to commit themselves and their organization at the outset to a programme of long-term behavioural change. This challenge can only be met by strong leadership.

LEADERSHIP QUALITY

The partnership development process is about change – change in strategy, change in service delivery, change in organizational structure. Change is a very unsettling process; even if those involved can appreciate the longer-term benefits of change they are inevitably concerned at how it will affect them personally. This is where leadership comes in. The choice of the leaders of a PPP is therefore a critically important issue; the leaders need to demonstrate the following characteristics:

PROMINENT POLITICAL PRESENCE

The creation of a PPP is a very political process – a partnership cannot succeed unless those leading the individual partners are committed to the process. This means that those involved in promoting and leading the partnership itself (the chair of the steering group, the partnership champion, the partnership chair and the executive director) must have an appropriate political presence. They have to understand the political pressures on the partners and to be able to deal with the leaders and members of the respective governing bodies on a relatively equal basis; they must also enjoy the support and confidence of the partner representatives on the board. A great deal of partnership working requires detailed networking and prediscussion which can only be achieved satisfactorily if those leading the partnership have the necessary political skills and strategic understanding.

STRONG INTERPERSONAL SKILLS

While political and networking skills may open doors they need to be backed up by strong interpersonal skills. The partnership leaders, while remaining committed to achieving the long-term strategic goals of the partnership, will have to have the ability to negotiate (and possibly compromise) with the individual partners on an almost daily basis. In addition there has to be an excellent relationship between the steering group chair and the partnership champion, and between the partnership chair and the executive director. Each pair has to work together as one and to trust each other implicitly. The champion and executive director also have to develop close working relations with the staff of partner organizations. Successful partnerships demand excellent interpersonal skills from their leaders and this characteristic is perhaps more important than a specialist knowledge of the partnership's subject area.

CONSISTENCY

A partnership is a long-term venture; for that reason it is important that there is a reasonable degree of consistency in the leadership arrangements. Changing a chair on an annual basis is not helpful to a partnership's cause; equally however, installing a chair for a lengthy period (say longer than three years) is not a healthy approach since this has the potential to demotivate some of the partners. Similar arguments apply at executive director level – five years, with a possible extension of two to three years, seems to be a reasonable approach. Every partnership will wish to develop their own solution but consistency of leadership makes an important contribution to success.

PARTNERSHIP VALUES

Most organizations see the benefit in adopting a set of values to underpin their work and public private partnerships are no different in this respect. However since the partners come from different sectors they bring with them somewhat different values and successful partnership working requires a certain amount of compromising between these values. It is therefore important to discuss and agree on a set of values at a fairly early stage in the partnership development process. The following values have been identified as being important by various commentators and those with practical experience of running PPPs.

OPENNESS AND TRUST

A commitment to partnership working can only be fostered if the partnership itself displays an openness in the way it conducts its affairs – 'open-book accounting' has to be taken to the extreme if a partnership is to be successful. Openness however is only the first step in the process – it is important that partners do not abuse that openness but use it as a basis to develop a trust in each other's activities and their contribution to the partnership. Once distrust enters into a relationship it is bound to fail. However it has to be recognized that the concept of openness is not an easy one to adopt – organizations tend to be secretive even within themselves and sharing potentially sensitive information with partners is difficult to encourage. It is made much easier if there is a local culture of openness but much will depend on the way the chair and executive director manage the partnership's business and on their relationships with the leaders and staff of the partners. As mutual confidence grows at the individual level so it becomes much easier for the partnership as a whole to become more transparent in its working and thus encourage trust between partners.

INTEGRITY AND FAIRNESS

Partners will find it difficult to trust one another unless they demonstrate integrity and fairness. It is important that each partner respects the integrity of the others and that they treat each other fairly. The point has already been made that a partnership should not impinge on a partner's own activities but should be adding value; it is equally true that partners within a partnership should take care not to use the 'cover' of partnership working to try and widen their own sphere of influence at the expense of the other partners. For example a learning partnership will include both HE and FE institutions; the partnership will doubtless be trying to encourage new forms of provision and it is important that the individual institutions are not tempted to stray into areas or types of provision already covered by another partner – the aim is to build on the strengths of each other and not to promote one at the expense of another. Respect for each other's contribution is an essential value for successful partnership working.

MUTUAL SUPPORT OVER RISKS AND REWARDS

It is inevitable that not every partner will gain equally from every initiative of the partnership; equally some will risk more than others in some activities. A very good test of partnership working is to see how partners react and support each other over the differential risks and rewards stemming from a partnership's work. While the contractual arrangements underpinning the work of some service delivery partnerships will reflect the agreed risk/reward balance the position is not so clear in many other types of partnerships. There may well be political risks (in a local authority sense) arising from some of the strategies that may be developed by say an economic partnership; it is incumbent on the other members of the partnership (such as the chamber of commerce in this example) to express public support for the council and help them in any way they can rather than to try and make political capital out of the situation. A successful partnership is one where the individual partners accept without question that there will be differential risks and rewards attached to everything which the partnership does and offer active support where appropriate. It is only in this way that the partnership as a whole can start to develop its own culture of risk taking which is so necessary to achieve the changes which the partnership will have been established to deliver.

BELIEF IN CULTURAL AND BEHAVIOURAL CHANGE

A PPP is about delivering long-term change; this cannot be done without achieving cultural and behavioural change in the individual partners. Indeed one of the key reasons for establishing a partnership is often the encouragement of cultural change in one partner by working with other types of organization – a particular stimulus for service delivery partnerships. The partners in a successful partnership will need to demonstrate a shared belief in cultural change; this is why the annual business plan should include a section on how the partners have changed the way they do business as a result of the partnership. For example the relationship between a chamber of commerce and its members should change as a result of its membership of a local strategic partnership. While continuing to represent their members' interests in an essentially selfish way they should also be seen to spend more time explaining public policy and encouraging positive private sector input into the strategy development process. Organizations in a borough or district which believe in partnership working are likely to demonstrate somewhat different characteristics than those in areas where this is not the norm (more inclusivity, consultation and adoption of common objectives).

OPERATIONAL AND MANAGEMENT STRUCTURES

The characteristics outlined in the previous sections are somewhat ephemeral in nature – they are essentially concerned with the ethos of partnership working rather than the nuts and bolts of partnership management. But clear objectives and a supportive ethos cannot of themselves create success; they have to be underpinned by the right sort of management structure and operational procedures. While many of the characteristics outlined below can apply to successful organizations of any type the unusual nature of partnership working adds a specific dimension to all of them.

THOROUGH PREPARATION AND PLANNING

All organizations benefit from thorough planning but it is particularly important for public private partnerships since they represent a relatively new way of doing things. By their nature they challenge a number of preconceptions and because of this their development cannot be rushed. It inevitably takes time to create something new which can enjoy the support of all the potential partners and stakeholders. The partnership development process outlined in the first part of this book may take years rather than months – an analysis of economic partnerships in the South East indicated that the average development stage lasted some 18 months from initial meetings to formal establishment, with some taking nearly three years. While the Government may sometimes impose a deadline for the establishment of a partnership there is generally no specific timescale – deadlines are self-imposed. There is therefore no reason why those involved in establishing a PPP (the steering group) should rush things. The key areas where it is essential to reach agreement at the start are set out in the partnership development strategy discussed earlier, and it will be difficult for a partnership to move forward with any confidence if it is constantly revisiting its purpose or structure. Time spent on this stage will be very well spent. The same principle of thorough planning is just as true once the partnership has been established; drafting the annual business plan and, more specifically, agreeing the annual output targets is a delicate process requiring time and effort. It is a very visible way of reinvigorating partners' commitment to the partnership and must not be rushed.

BALANCED MEMBERSHIP

A partnership cannot be a true partnership if there is a perception that it is dominated by one partner. While it may well be true that one partner or sector provides most of the resources – for example in the health sector – it is important for the credibility of the partnership that the other partners do not see themselves as second class or just there to make up the numbers. They must feel that their contribution is making a difference; if not they will rapidly lose interest. One of the marks of a successful chair is the way in which they encourage the involvement of all the partners and generate a partnership feeling round the table.

AGREED ACCOUNTABILITY

The problems of establishing a proper accountability framework for a partnership have been discussed in Chapter 7. It is important that the partners give specific consideration to the accountability issues at an early stage in the development process. There is a very real danger that, unless there is overt agreement on what is meant by accountability and how it is to be managed, the individual partners will presume that their own interpretation is shared by others. Democratic accountability is a particular issue which becomes increasingly important as a partnership matures and starts to attract and spend resources whether from the public or private purse; in the enthusiasm of partnership working it can sometimes be overlooked that a partnership board is not democratically elected and accountability for public funds is a potential minefield unless the principles are agreed beforehand.

CLEAR BUSINESS PLANS

The importance of clarity of objectives and thorough planning has already been emphasized. It follows that a successful partnership needs to express this through the business planning process. Both the strategic plan and the annual business plan need to be very public statements of a PPP's objectives and programmes; they therefore need to be very clear and specific with easily identifiable targets so that the wider stakeholder group, and not just the partners themselves, can develop confidence in the partnership's work.

REGULAR PERFORMANCE REVIEWS

As pointed out in Chapter 8 it is of little value to publish grandiose plans and targets unless achievement of these is monitored and reported to the wider stakeholder community; if corrective action is required then that also needs to be publicized. To be successful a partnership has to demonstrate that, not only can it set demanding targets, but that an effective feedback and control system is also in place. It is in this way that it can build up credibility with the wider community.

EXCELLENT WORKING RELATIONSHIPS WITH AND BETWEEN PARTNERS

Such an integrated planning and control system can only work if there are good working relationships between the staff of the partnership and the individual partners, and between the partners. Such relationships can only be built on a foundation of trust and shared values.

RESOURCE CONTINUITY

Since PPPs are engaged in a long-term process it follows that it is important that the partnership has a reasonable certainty over the level of available resources. While there will always be difficulties – no organization can guarantee resources ad infinitum – it is incumbent on the partners to back up their commitment with some certainty over resources. A rolling three-year horizon is probably the best that can be hoped for. A useful approach to this issue is to try and develop some initial funding principles at the outset (for example every partner or sector to contribute a specific percentage of a partnership's agreed minimum operating costs over the next three years). A successful partnership which is perceived to have delivered on its objectives should be able to negotiate reasonable resource guarantees from its partners; an alternative is to try and build up some reserves of its own but this is a dangerous policy – a partnership should not be developing a 'life of its own' and holding on to funds which could be more properly used by the partners themselves.

A PPP which can tick most of the boxes shown in Figure 9.1 will be successful. Such partnerships are likely to become more and more prevalent over the next few years; the trend towards the closer integration between the public and private sectors to deliver improved public policy and services will undoubtedly continue to accelerate and it is important that public private partnerships, as the organizational means to deliver this overall strategy, should become more effective and responsive in the way they work. However it is not easy to establish a robust partnership – considerable time and effort is required to build up the culture of mutual confidence and self-interest which is so essential for successful partnership working.

Purpose and objectives	*Leadership quality*	*Partnership values*	*Management*
• Clear objectives • Specific added value • Long-term commitment	• Prominent political presence • Strong inter-personal skills • Consistency	• Openness and trust • Integrity and fairness • Mutual support • Shared belief in cultural change	• Thorough planning • Balanced membership • Agreed accountability • Clear business plans • Regular performance reviews • Excellent working relationships • Continuity of resource

Figure 9.1   Characteristics of successful partnerships

References

The following organizations are useful sources of information on public private partnerships:

Forum for the Future	www.forumforthefuture.org.uk
HM Treasury	www.hm-treasury.gov.uk
Improvement and Development Agency	www.idea.gov.uk
Institute for Public Policy Research	www.ippr.org.uk
Local Government Association	www.lga.gov.uk
New Local Government Network	www.nlgn.org.uk
Office of the Deputy Prime Minister	www.odpm.gov.uk
Office of Government Commerce	www.ogc.gov.uk
Ourpartnership	www.ourpartnership.org.uk
Partnerships UK	www.partnershipsuk.org.uk
Public Private Partnerships Programme (4Ps)	www.4Ps.co.uk

Index

accountability 95–103, 113, 129–30
  community 102–3
  financial 99–102
  legal 99–102
  managerial 98–9
  political 96–8
added value 124–5
annual output targets 120–21

behavioural change 128
boards of partnerships 69–73
business planning 30
business plans 86–8, 89, 129–30

central government, as partner 36–7
chair of partnership 105
  appointment 67–9
  role 66–7, 68
  term of office 67
chambers of commerce 43
'Childcare' Partnerships 10
commercially based partnerships 12–14, 21
  economic benefits 21–2
  membership 64
  synergy potential 21–2
communication by partnerships 103–9
  operational 108
community accountability 102–3
community sector, as partner 42
company structure for partnerships 52–4
Crime and Community Safety Partnerships 9–10
cultural change 128

drivers for partnerships
  founder partners 24–5
  key individuals 26–7
  potential partners 25–6

economic benefits for partnerships 21–2
Education Action Zone Partnerships 10–11
education sector, as partner 41–2

Environmentally Oriented Partnerships 12
executive directors of partnerships 74–5, 105

financial accountability 99–102
funding agencies 21

governance of partnerships 70
Government Offices (GOs) 37–8

Health Action Zone Partnerships 10–11
health community, as partner 40–41

infrastructure of partnerships 73–6

leadership 125–6
Learning and Skills Council (LSC), as partner 38–9
legal accountability 99–102
Lifelong Learning Partnerships (LLPs) 41
Local Authorities, as partner 39–40
local authority companies 54
Local Economic Partnerships 12
Local Health Forums 11
Local Learning Partnerships 12
Local Strategic Partnerships 10

management of partnerships 79–93
  principles 80–81
  process 81–4
managerial accountability 98–9
Milton Keynes (UK), strategic partnerships 4–5

negotiation with stakeholders 46–7
New Deal Strategic Partnerships 11
newsletters 106–8

open-book accounting 23
operational management of partnerships 88–93
outcome targets 120

partnering, definition 1

partners 130
  central government 36–7
  characteristics 35–48
  community sector 42
  education sector 41–2
  health community 40–41
  Learning and Skills Council (LSC) 38–9
  local authorities 39–40
  long-term commitment 125
  private sector 42–3
  process management targets 114–15
  regional agencies 37–8
  reports to 106
  Small Business Service (SBS) 38–9
  voluntary sector 42
partnership champions 17–18
  appointment 32, 33
  identification 27–31
  role 28–9
  skills 29–31
partnership deeds 51–2
partnership lifecycle 17–20
partnerships
  accountability 55, 95–103, 113, 129
  added value 124–5
  agenda 81–4
  boards of 69–73
  business plans 86–8, 89
  chair of 66–9, 105
  characteristics of partners 35–48
  characteristics of successful 123–31
  communication 103–9
  company structure 52–4
  consequential action 18
  contextual factors 23
  delivery 18
  development time 19–20
  drivers 24–7
  establishment process 19–24
  executive directors 74–5, 105
  executive powers 54
  formal 51–2
  governance 70
  implementation 18
  independence 55
  infrastructure 73–6
  initiation 17
  interim structure 17, 31–3
  leadership quality 125–6

management of 79–93
management structures 128–31
membership 61–6, 129
operational management 88–93
operational structures 128–31
organizational structure 49–58
  options 54–8
outcomes 114
outputs 114
rationale for 22
resources 55, 76, 130–31
staffing 75
strategic objectives 124–5
strategic plans 84–6
strategy 18
success criteria 23–4
value for money 115–16
values 126–8
performance reviews 130
PFI (Private Finance Initiative) 6, 13
political accountability 96–8
Primary Care Trusts 40
Private Finance Initiative (PFI) 6, 13
private sector
  as partner 42–3
  public services involvement 6–8
project managers 27 *see also* partnership
    champions
public meetings 108
public private partnerships *see also*
    partnerships
  categories of 8–14
  definition 1–2
  historical background 2–6
  overseas 6, 7
public project partnerships 14
public services, private sector involvement 6–8

regeneration partnerships 11
regional agencies, as partner 37–8
Regional Development Agencies (RDAs) 37–8

seminars 108
service delivery partnerships 13
Small Business Service (SBS), as partner 38–9
specific service delivery coordination bodies
    12
staffing of partnerships 75
stakeholder maps 44–6

stakeholders
   classification 65
   negotiation 46–7
statutory based partnerships 9–11, 20–21
   membership 63–4
steering groups 31–2
strategic objectives of partnerships 124–5
strategic plans 84–6
strategic targets 120
success criteria 23–4
synergy potential for partnerships 21–2

targets
   annual output 120–21

characteristics 116–19
outcome 120
reporting system 119–21
setting 111–16
strategic 120
teamworking 30
Transport Partnerships 11

value for money 115–16
voluntary based partnerships 12, 21
   membership 64
voluntary sector, as partner 42

websites 106–8

About the Author

MICHAEL GEDDES

Michael Geddes is a practical manager with a particular interest in developing new organizational structures and ways of working across all sectors. He started his career at Cranfield Institute of Technology (now University) where he was responsible for introducing a coordinated planning process, integrating academic, financial and physical aspects into a coherent whole; he was also responsible for managing Cranfield's relationship with the Department of Education and Science. He played a key role in the assimilation of the National College of Agricultural Engineering at Silsoe into Cranfield, and led the process which resulted in Cranfield being awarded the contract by the Ministry of Defence to manage the Royal Military College of Science at Shrivenham, both major organizational challenges.

He moved to Ashridge in 1984 as Director of Administration and was responsible for reorganizing the Trust's activities through the creation of various separate but inter-linked companies. He also developed an interest in the leadership of multi-disciplinary project teams, particularly those involved in organizational change, and was the co-author of *Project Leadership* (first published by Gower in 1990). In 1990 he became one of the first non civil servants to be appointed a Chief Executive designate of a Next Steps agency; in that capacity he was responsible for turning a very traditional part of the civil service (the Civil Service Commission) into a financially self-supporting agency (Recruitment and Assessment Services). Unusually he combined this executive role with a regulatory function as a Civil Service Commissioner. The completion of the recruitment changes in 1995, under which the regulatory and executive functions were finally separated, led to his resignation from the post of Chief Executive but he remained a Commissioner for another couple of years in order to help the new commissioner structure to bed down.

From the mid-1990s he worked as an independent consultant; in addition to advising a number of government departments and overseas governments on appropriate organizational structures and senior appointments, he spent about half his time on the creation of the Milton Keynes Economic Partnership, one of the first genuine multi-sector partnerships, which was established to coordinate the strategic development of the area. By the time of his formal retirement at the end of 2003 the originally informal partnership had become a company with a number of subsidiaries.

He played a key role in the establishment of regional structures following the 1997 election and served for four years as the Vice Chairman of the Regional Assembly representing the economic partners; he also chaired the group of organizations set up to create the Oxford Cambridge Arc, an economic initiative to underpin the long-term development of the South Midlands. Although now formally retired he continues to provide ad hoc consultancy services and runs occasional seminars. He can be contacted at michael@mdgeddes.fsnet.co.uk.